I0474402

Real World Colouring Book

For Advanced Users & Adults

50 Images

Created From Real Life Photos For You To Colour As You Please.

ISBN 978-0-359-93600-7

90000

9 780359 936007

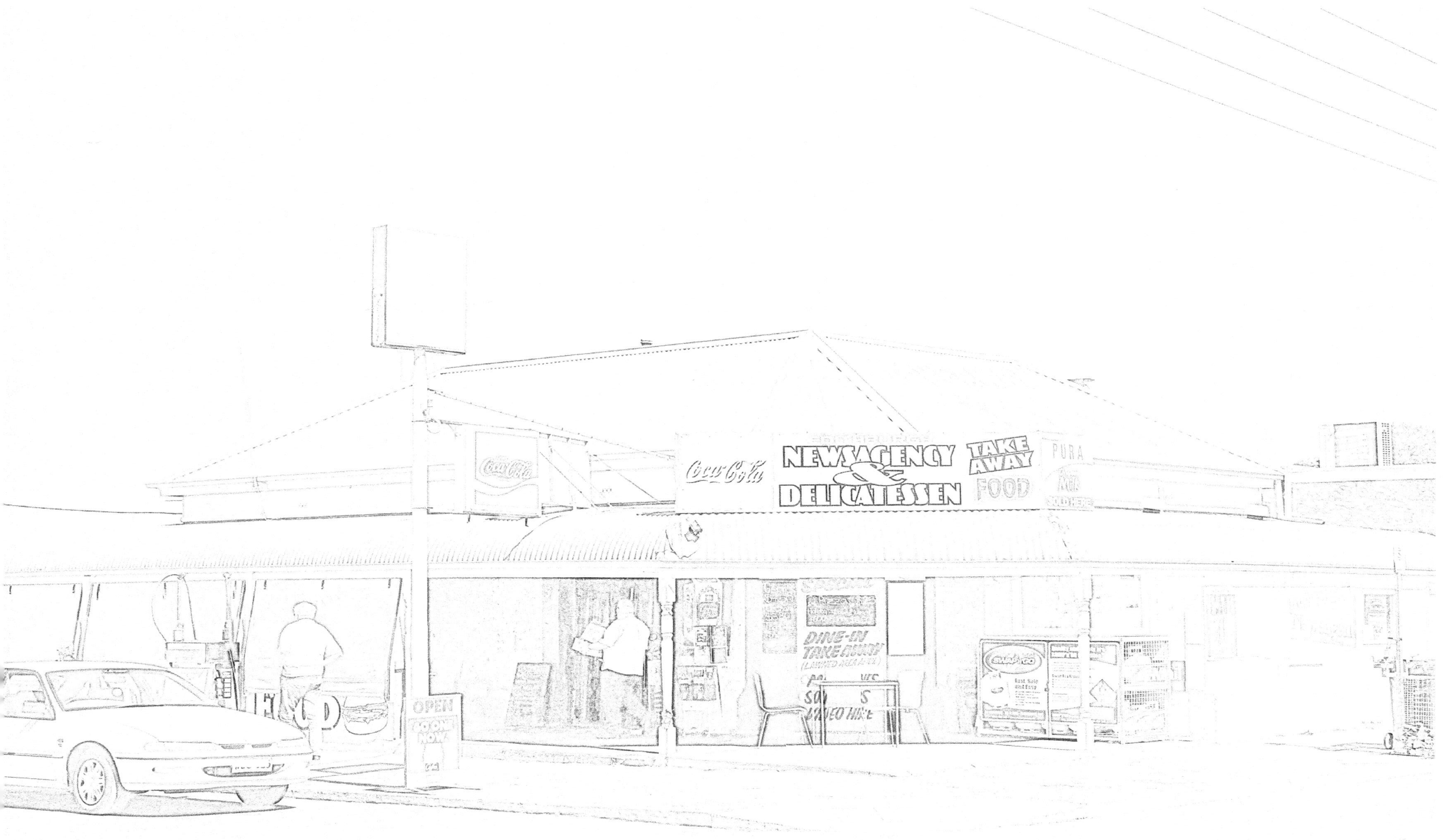
Coca-Cola
NEWSAGENCY & DELICATESSEN
TAKE AWAY
FOOD
PURA
Coca-Cola
DINE-IN
TAKE AWAY
OPEN
FOOD

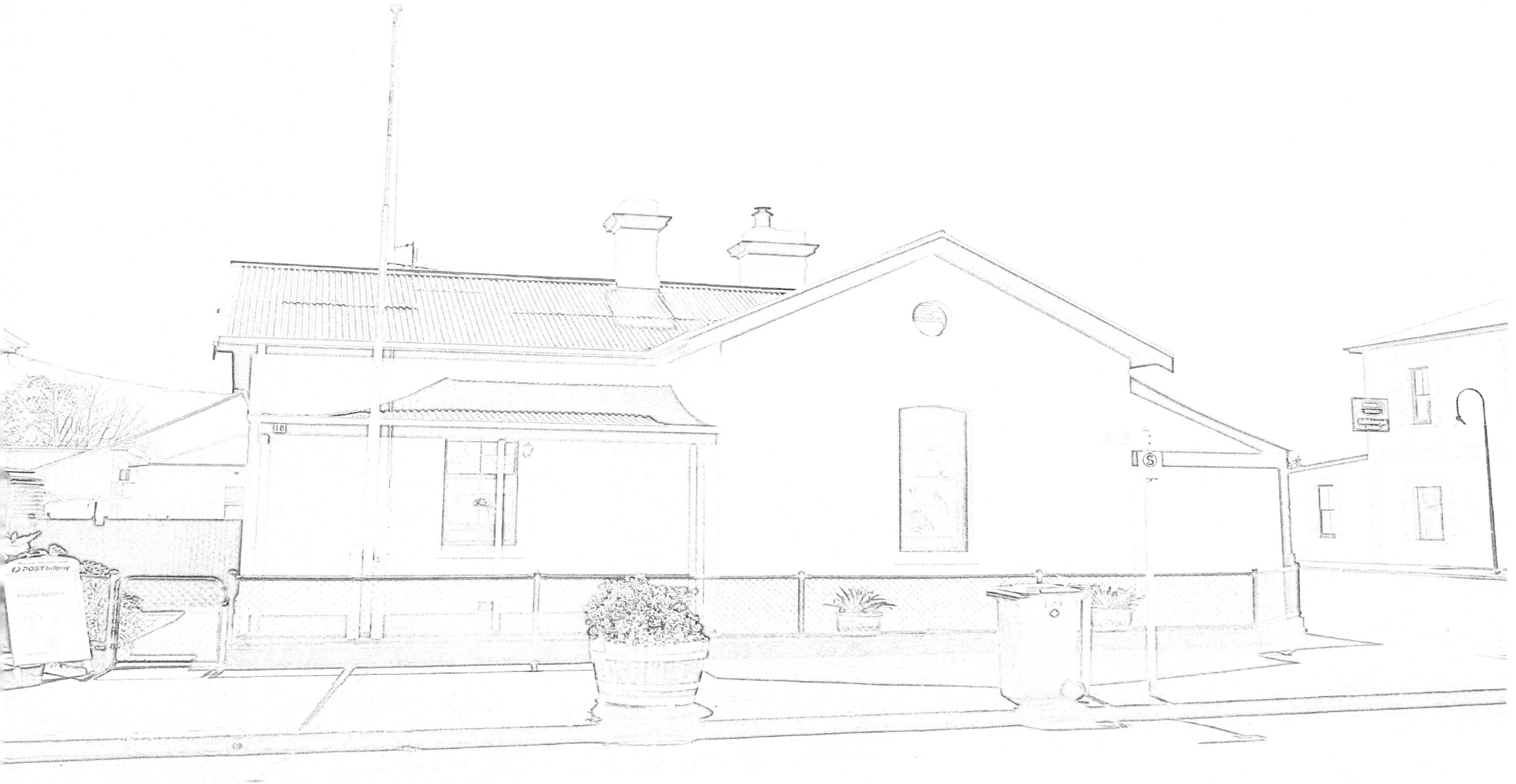
POST billpay

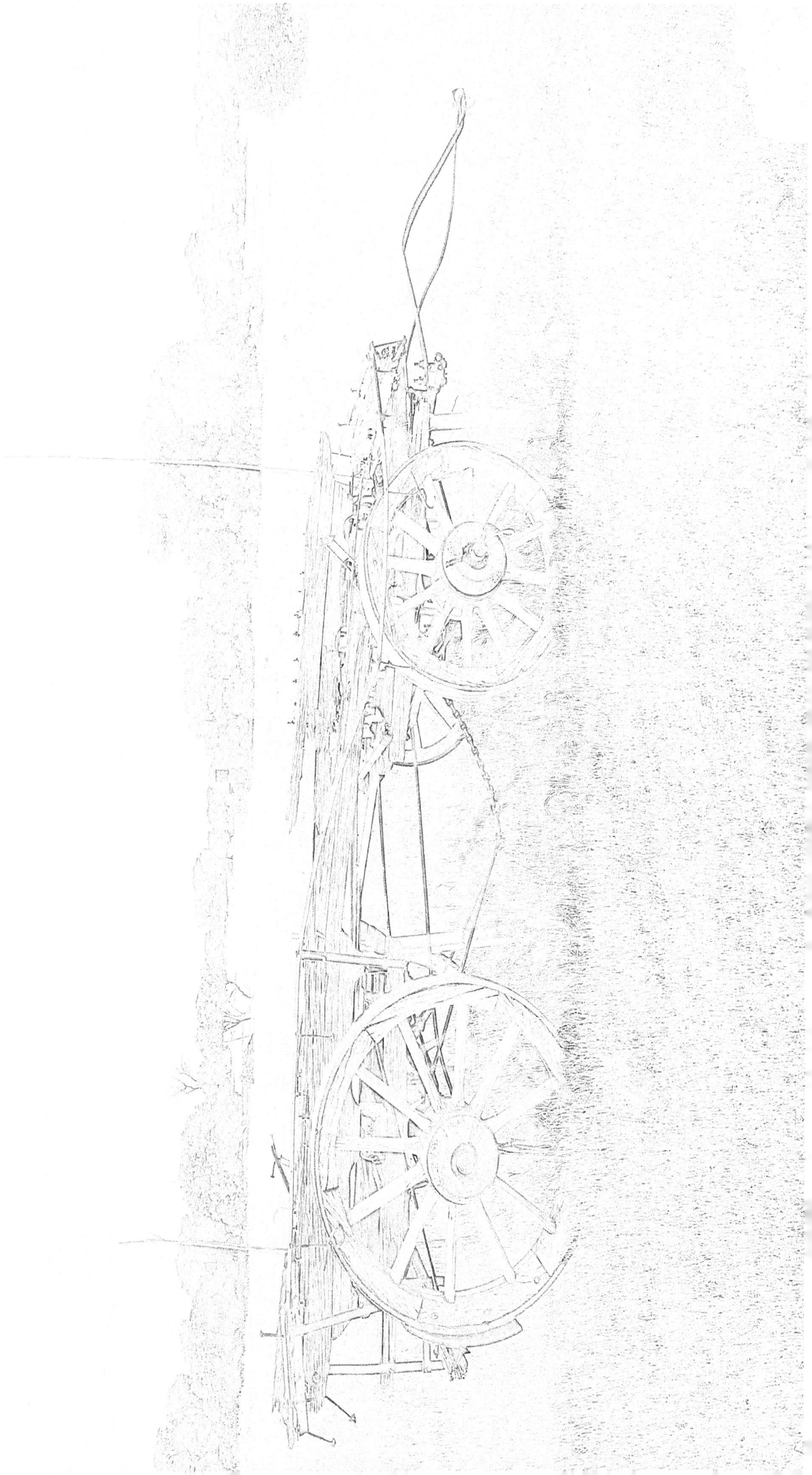

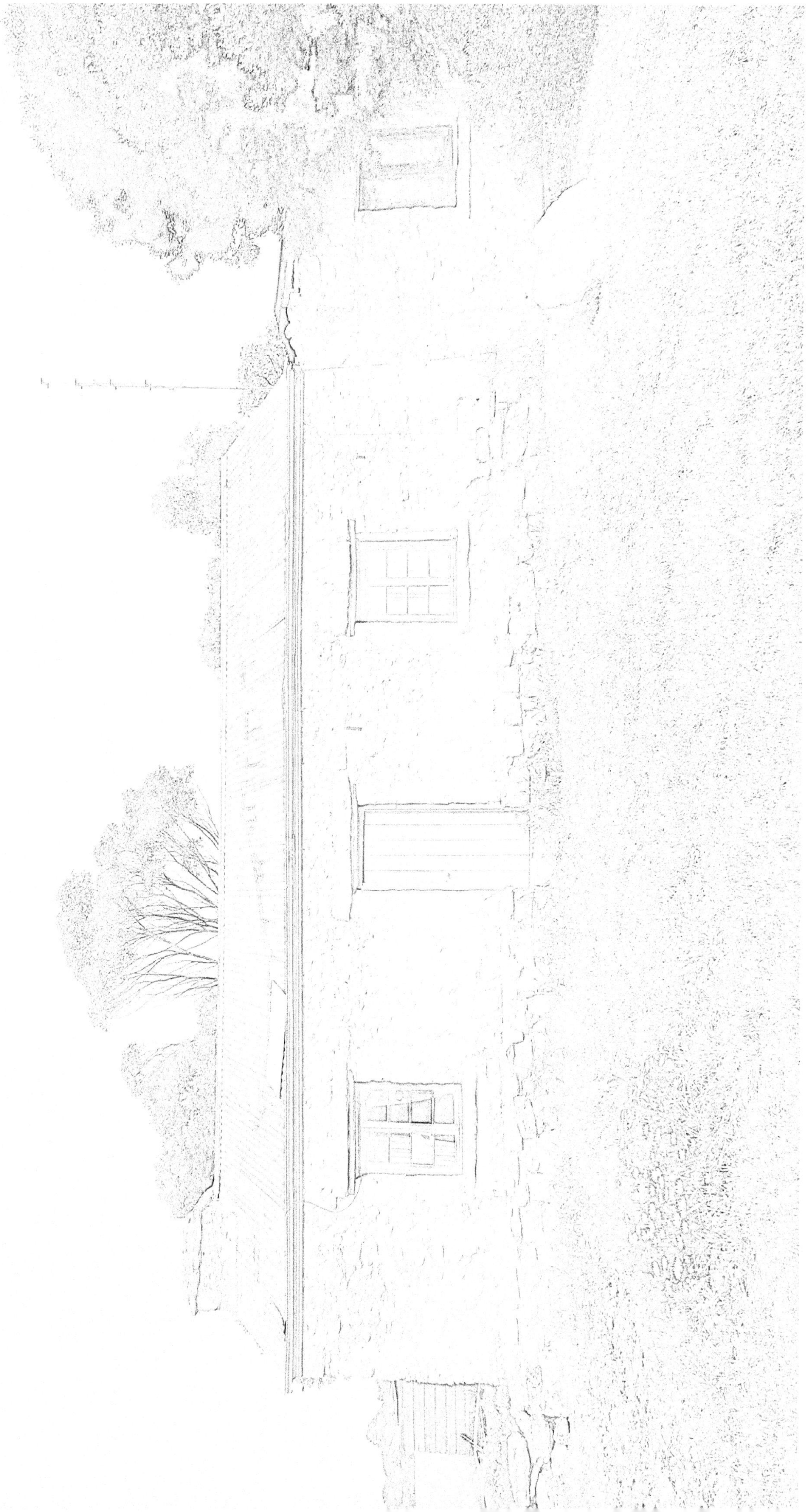

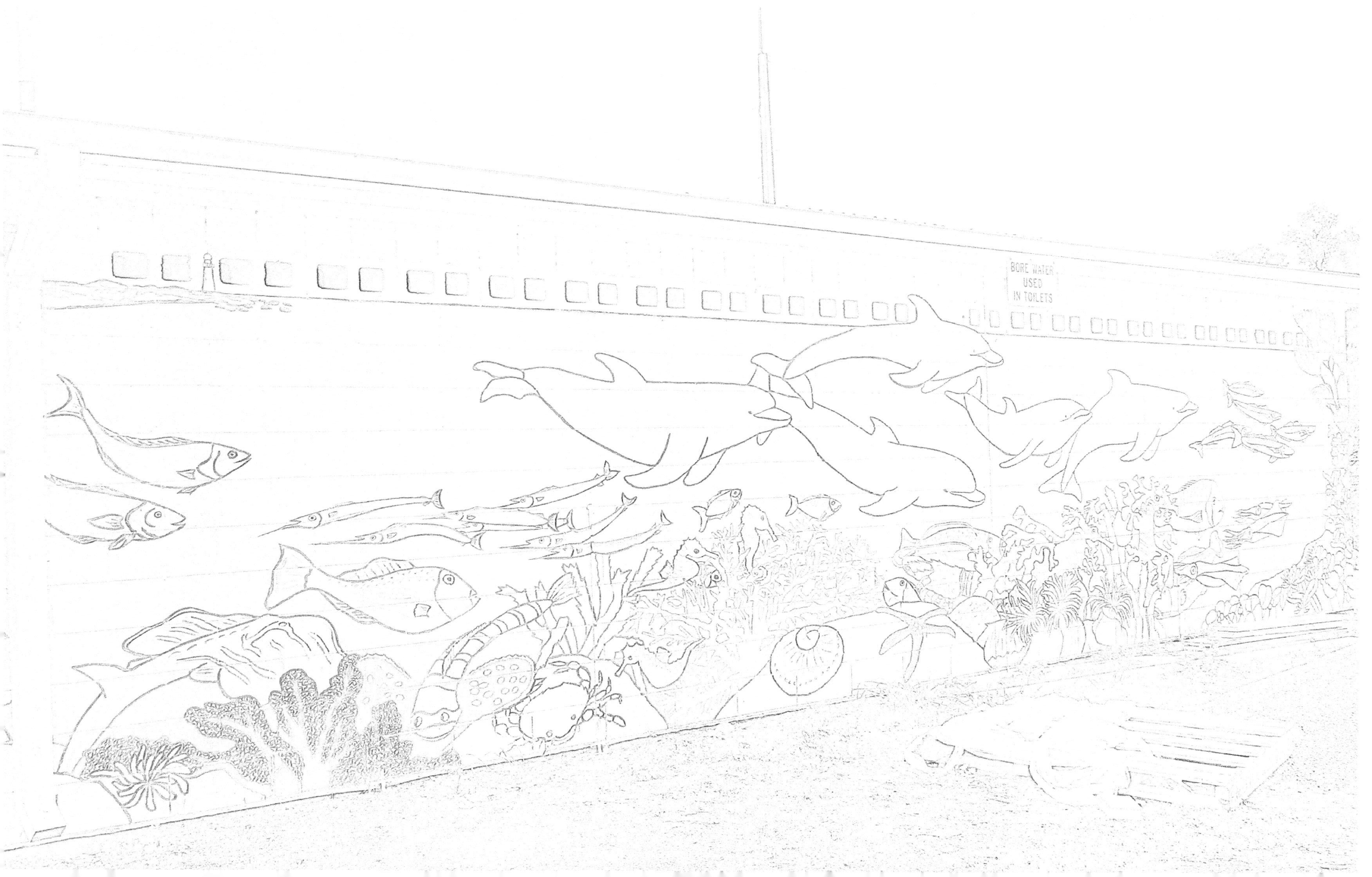
BORE WATER
USED
IN TOILETS

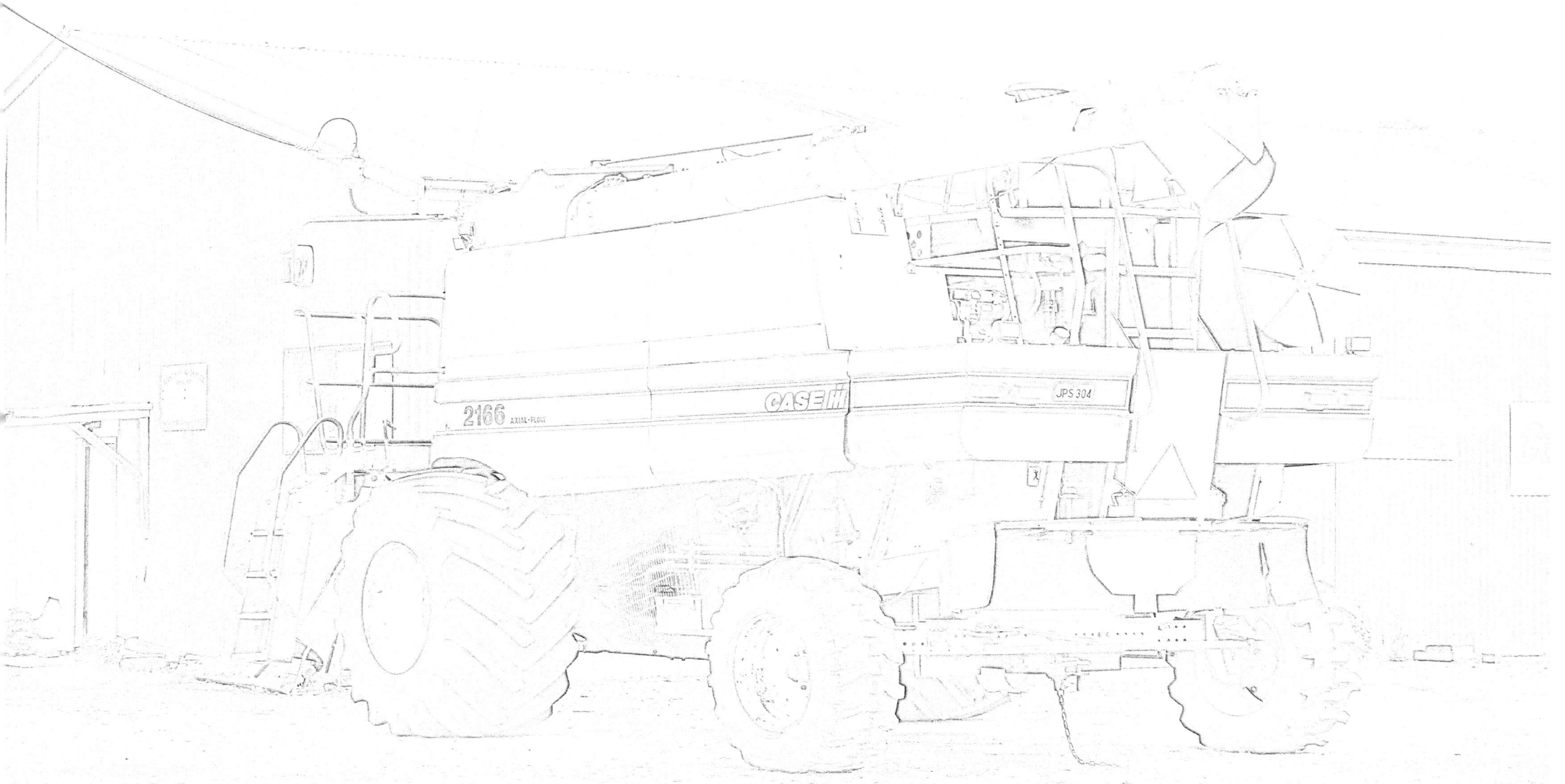
2166 AXIAL-FLOW
CASE IH
JPS 304

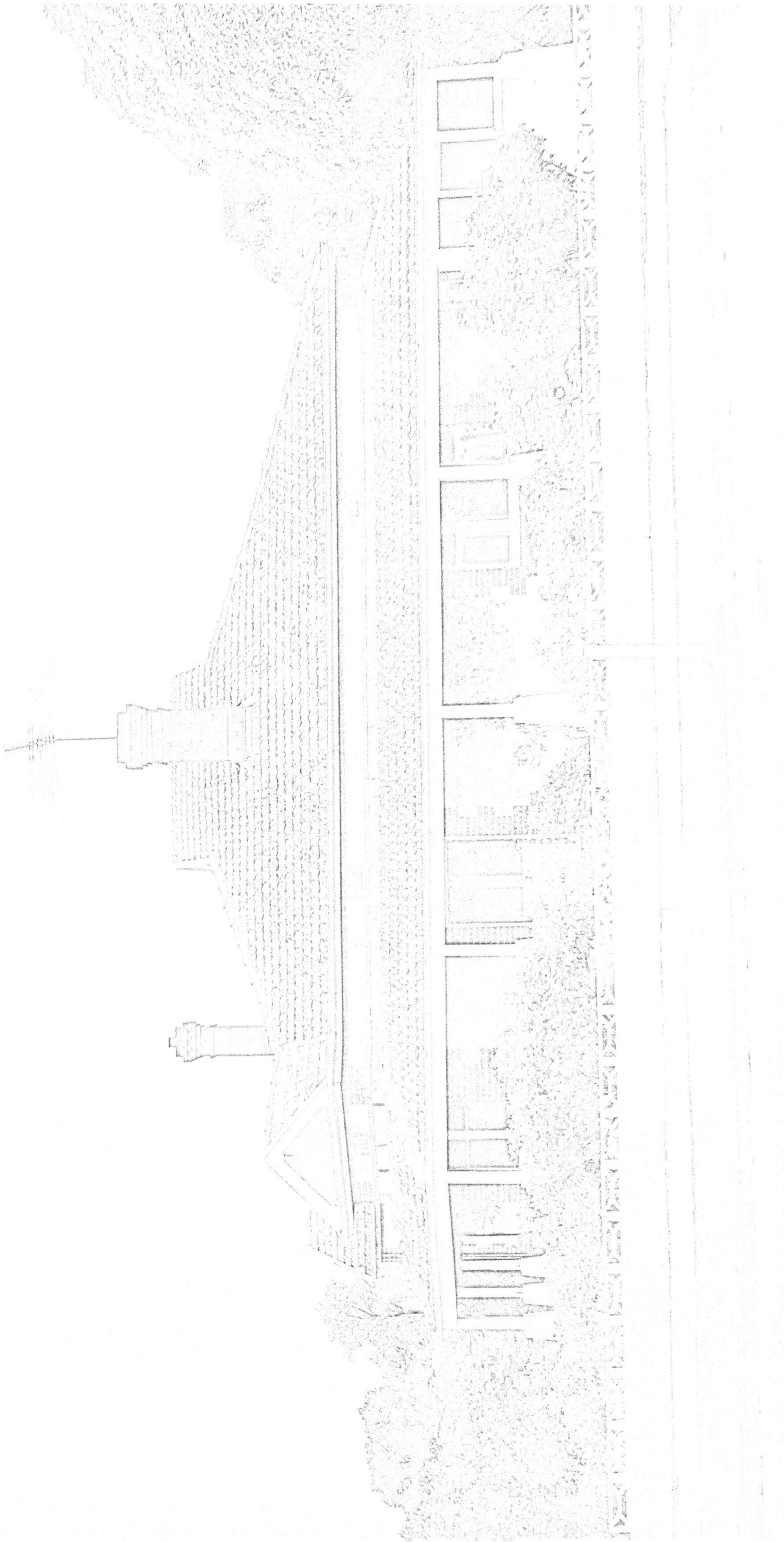

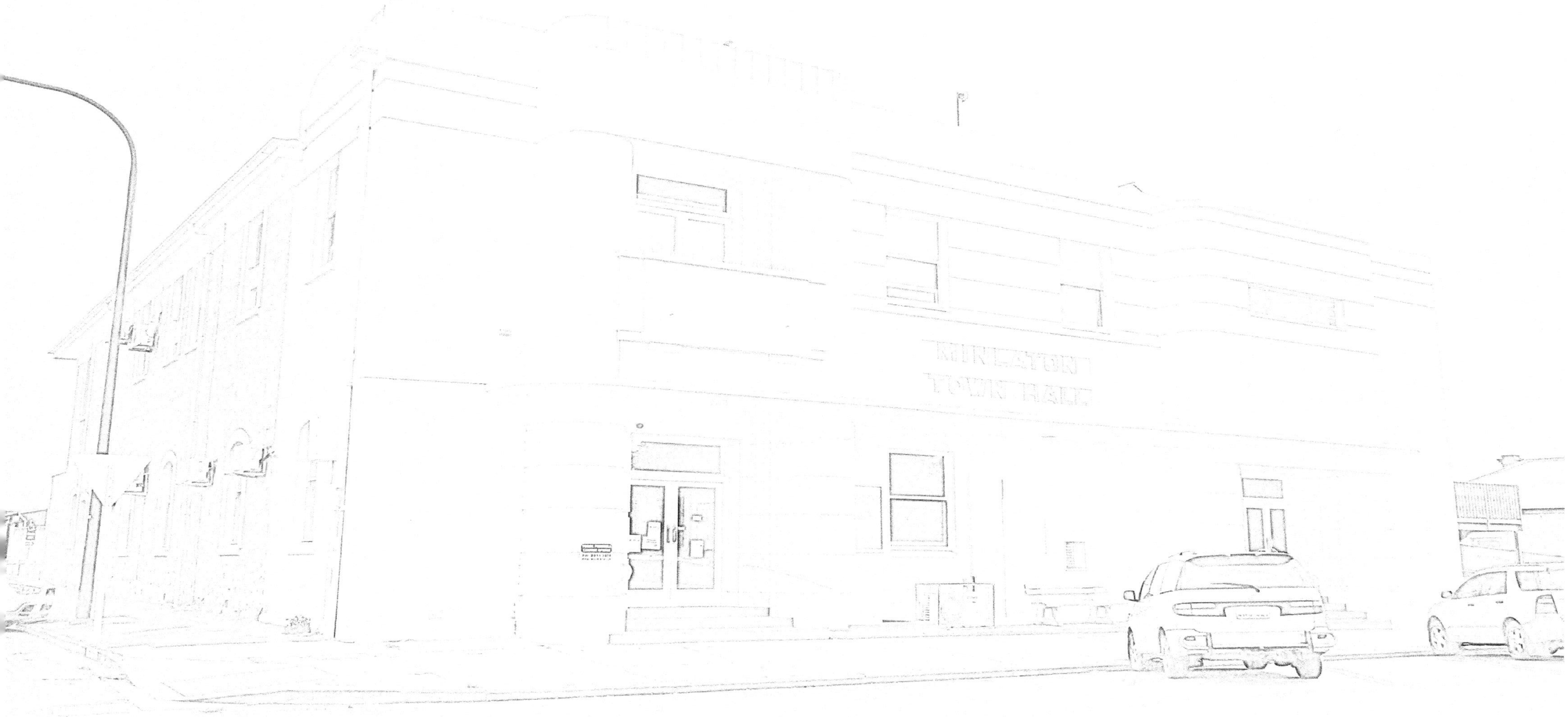
MINLATON
TOWN HALL

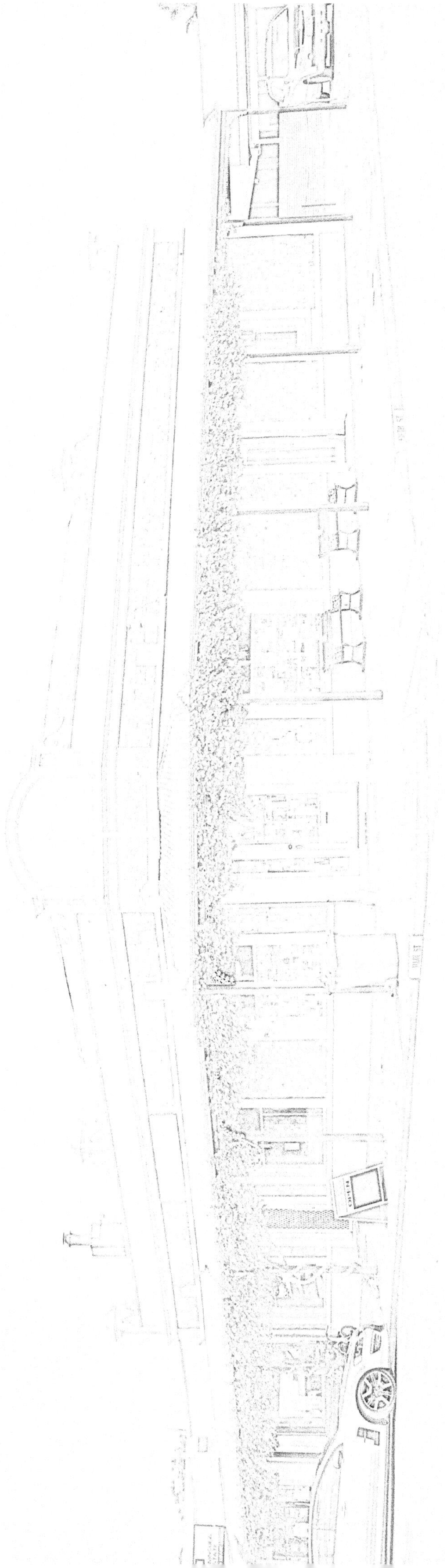

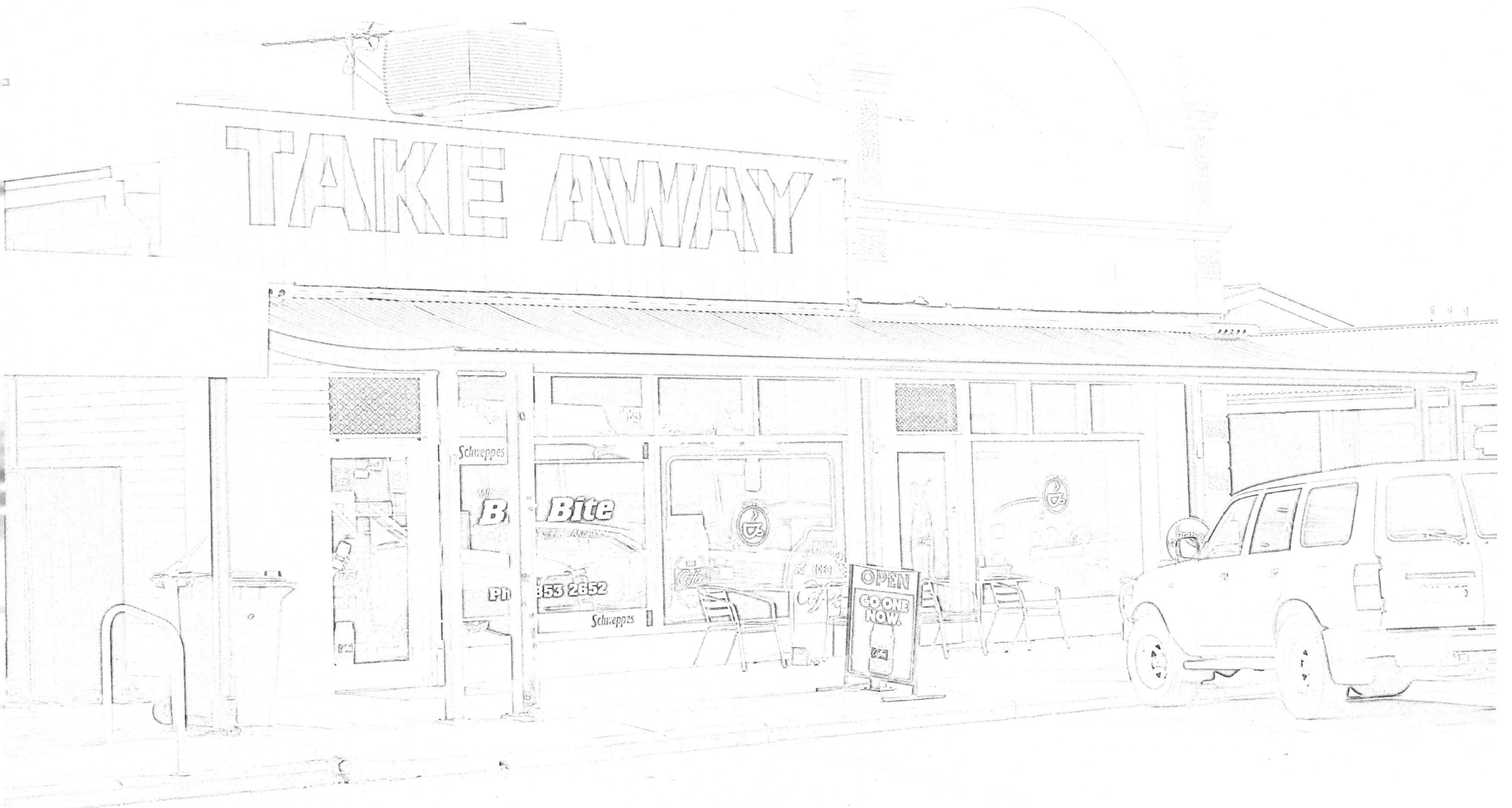
TAKE AWAY
Schweppes
Bite
Ph 853 2652
Schweppes
OPEN
GO ONE NOW.

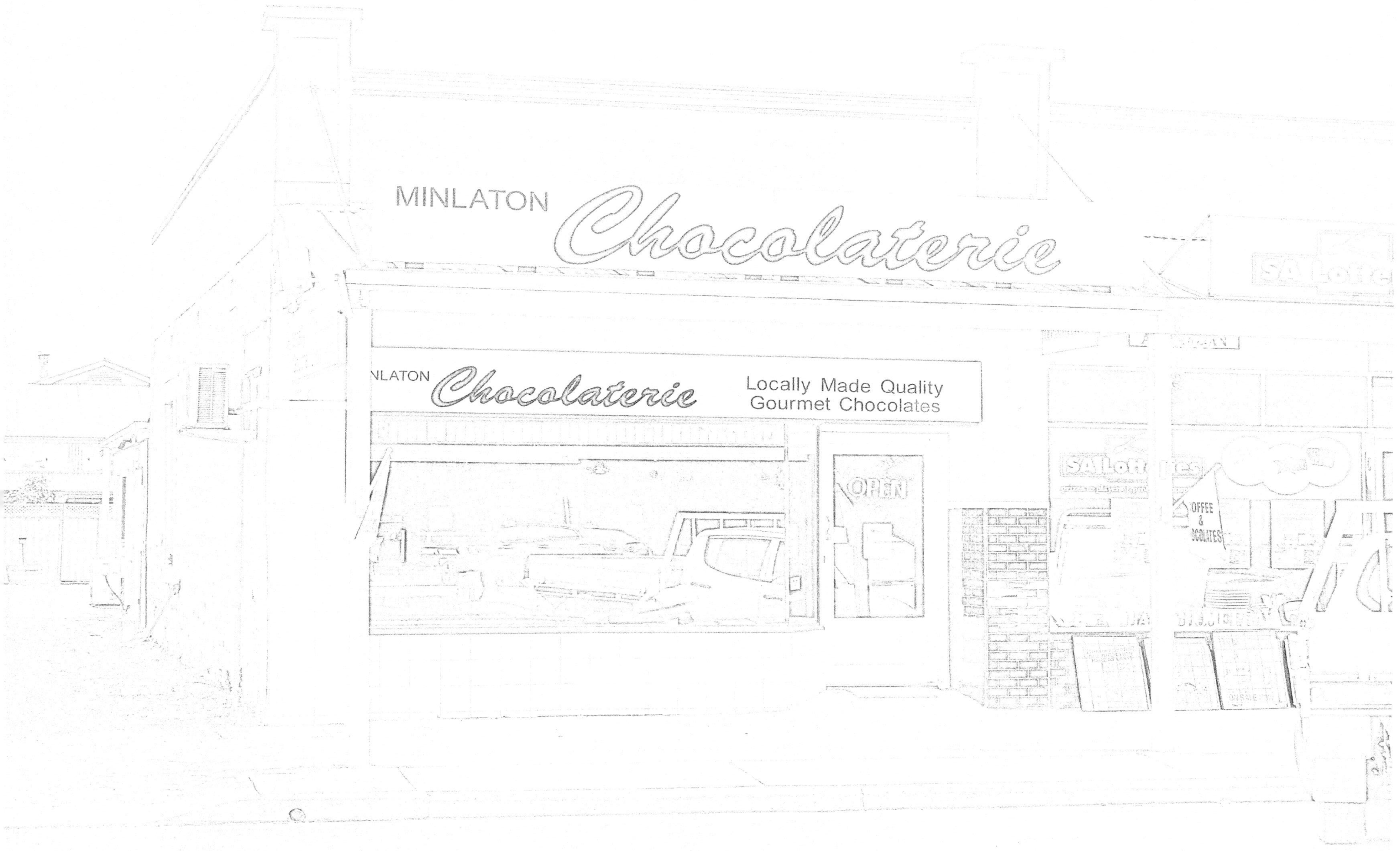

MINLATON Chocolaterie
NLATON Chocolaterie
Locally Made Quality
Gourmet Chocolates
OPEN
SA Lotte
OFFEE
&
OCOLATES

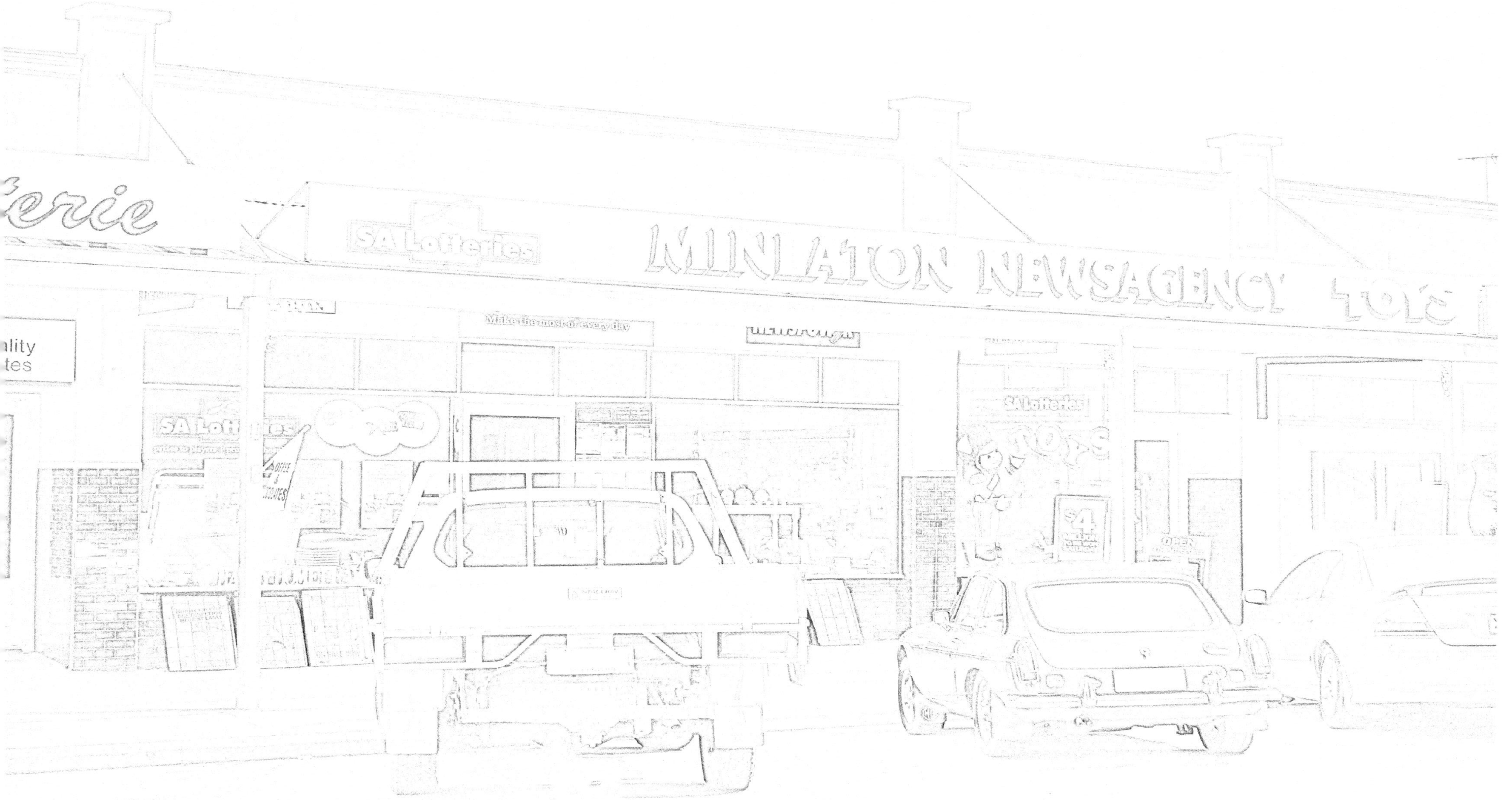

erie
SA Lotteries
MINLATON NEWSAGENCY TOYS
Make the most of every day
ality
tes
SA Lotteries
TOYS
$4
OPEN

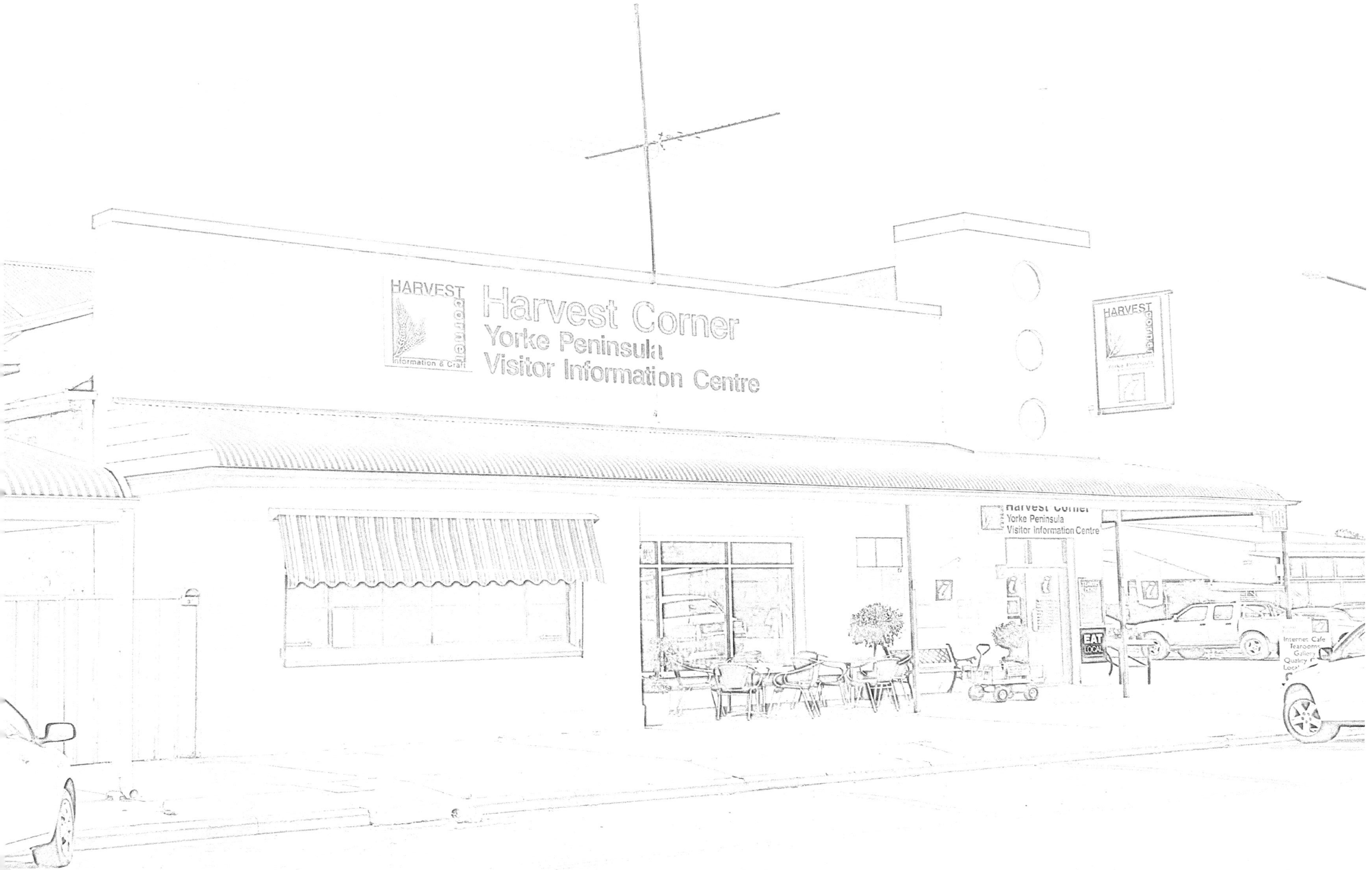
HARVEST
corner
Information & Craft
Harvest Corner
Yorke Peninsula
Visitor Information Centre
HARVEST
corner
Harvest Corner
Yorke Peninsula
Visitor Information Centre
EAT
LOCAL

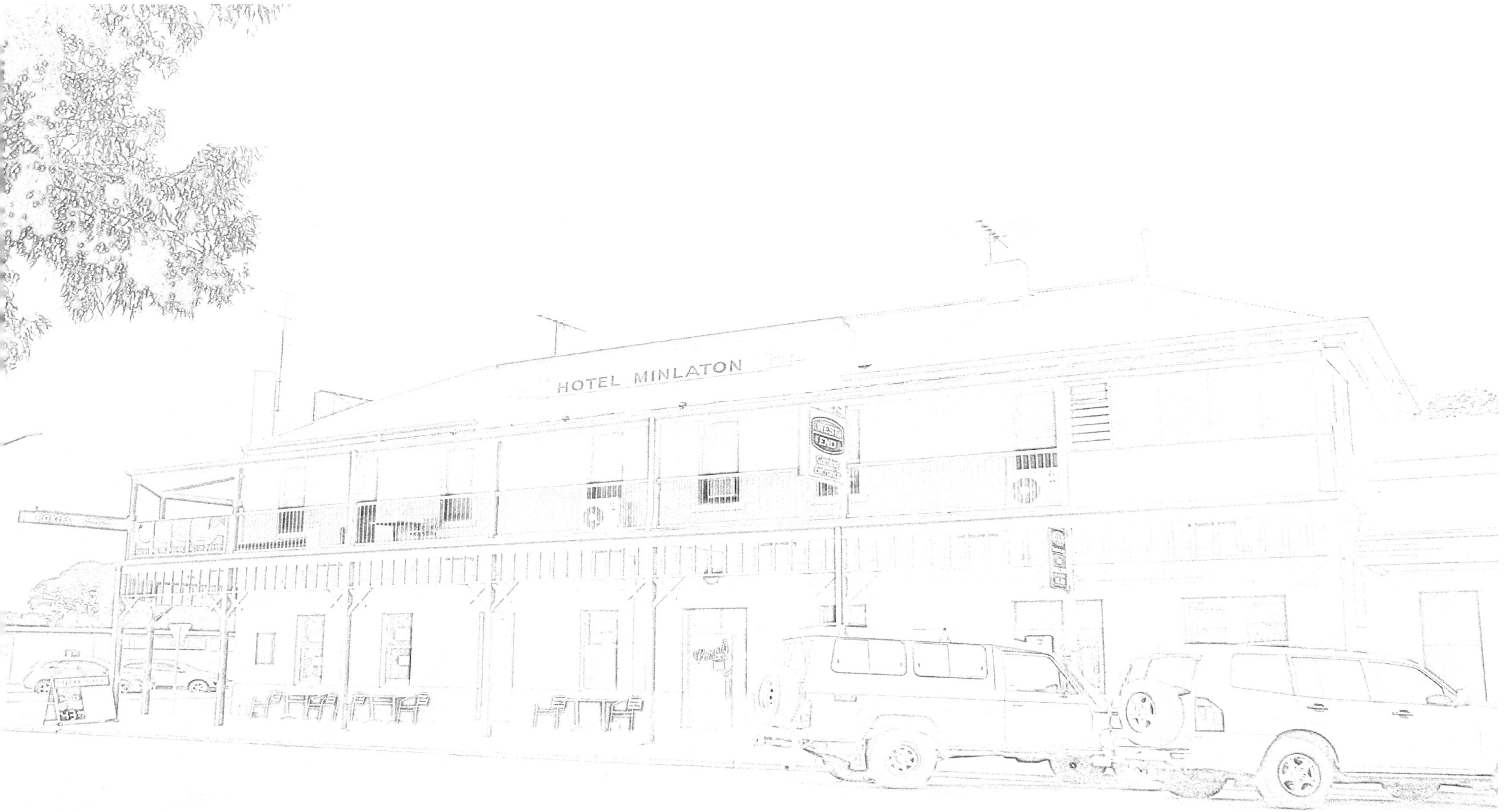
HOTEL MINLATON
WEST END

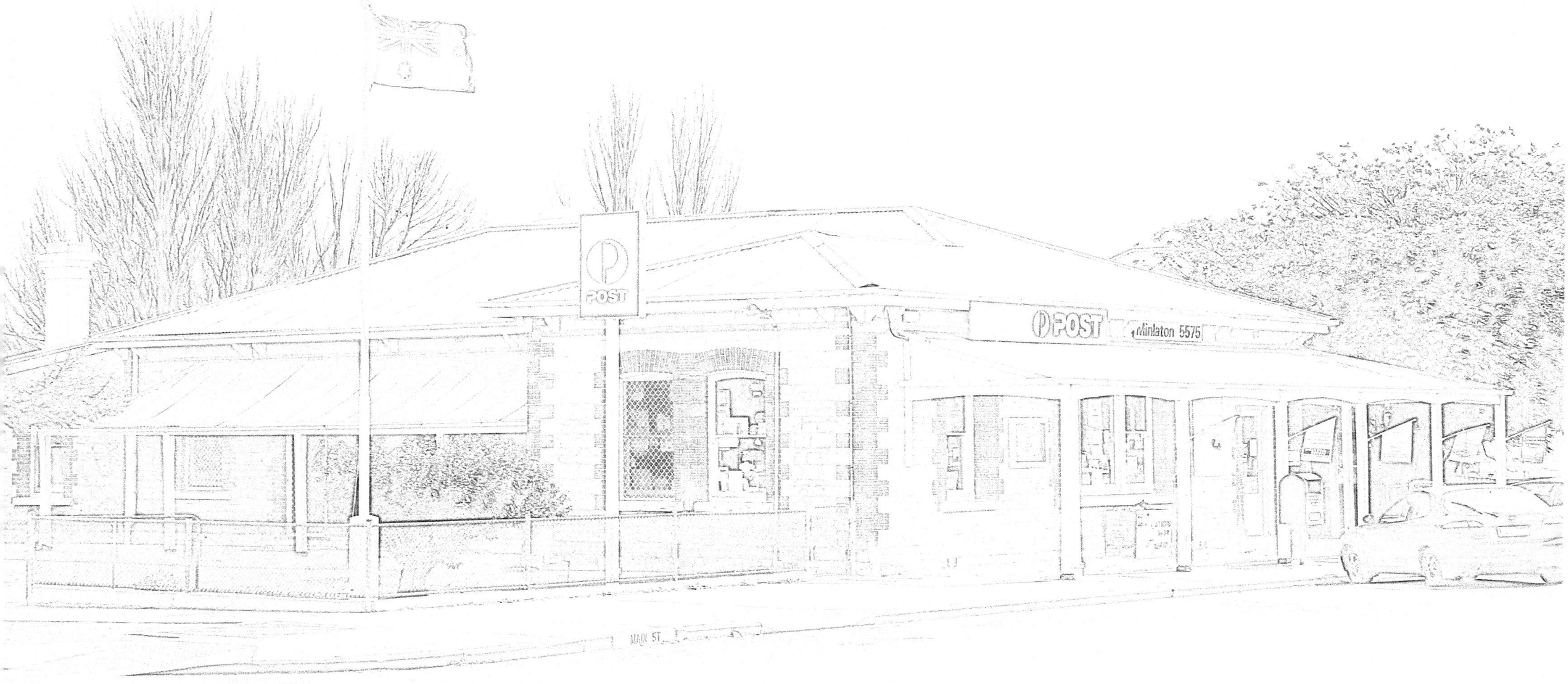
POST
POST
Minlaton 5575
MAIN ST.

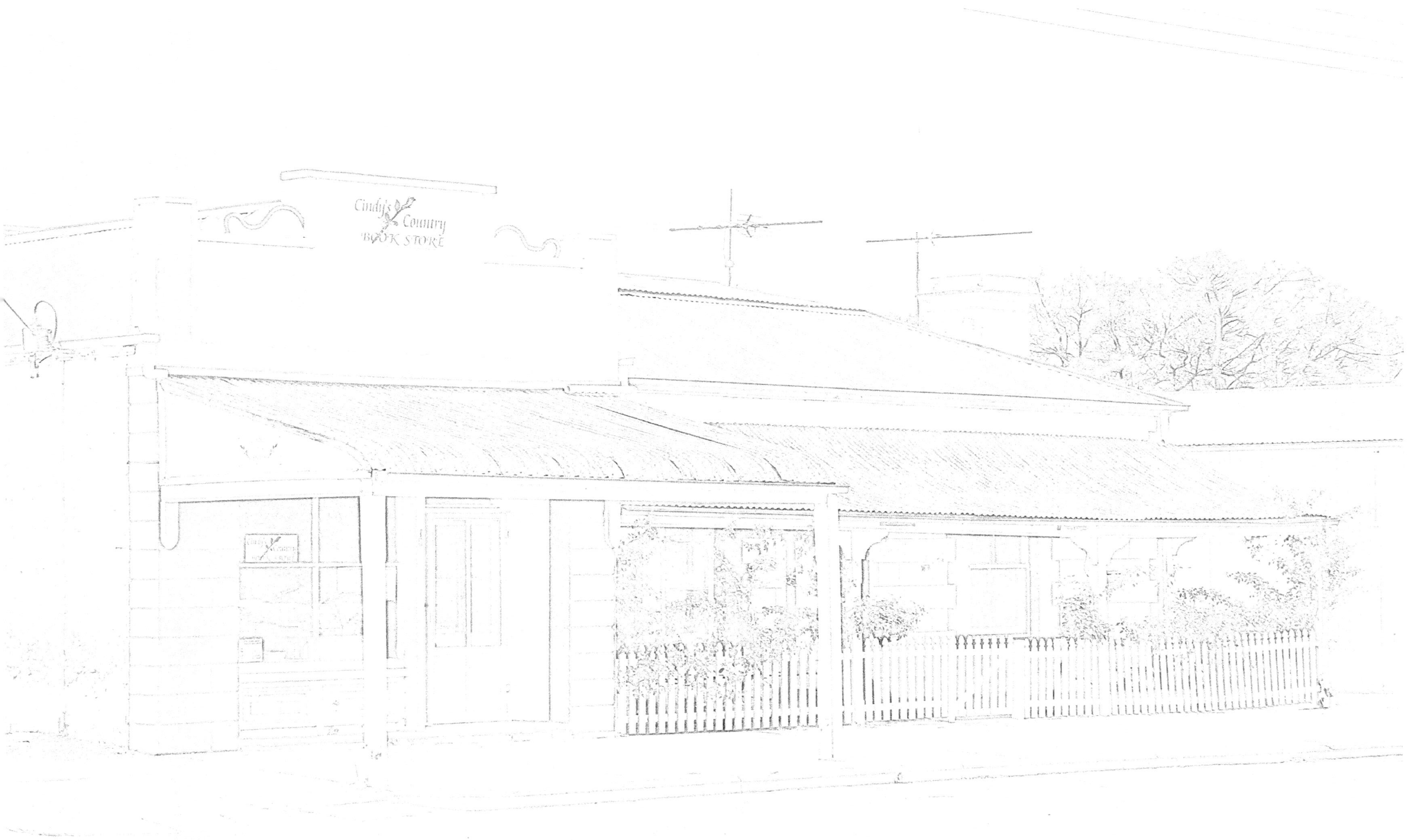
Cindy's Country
BOOK STORE

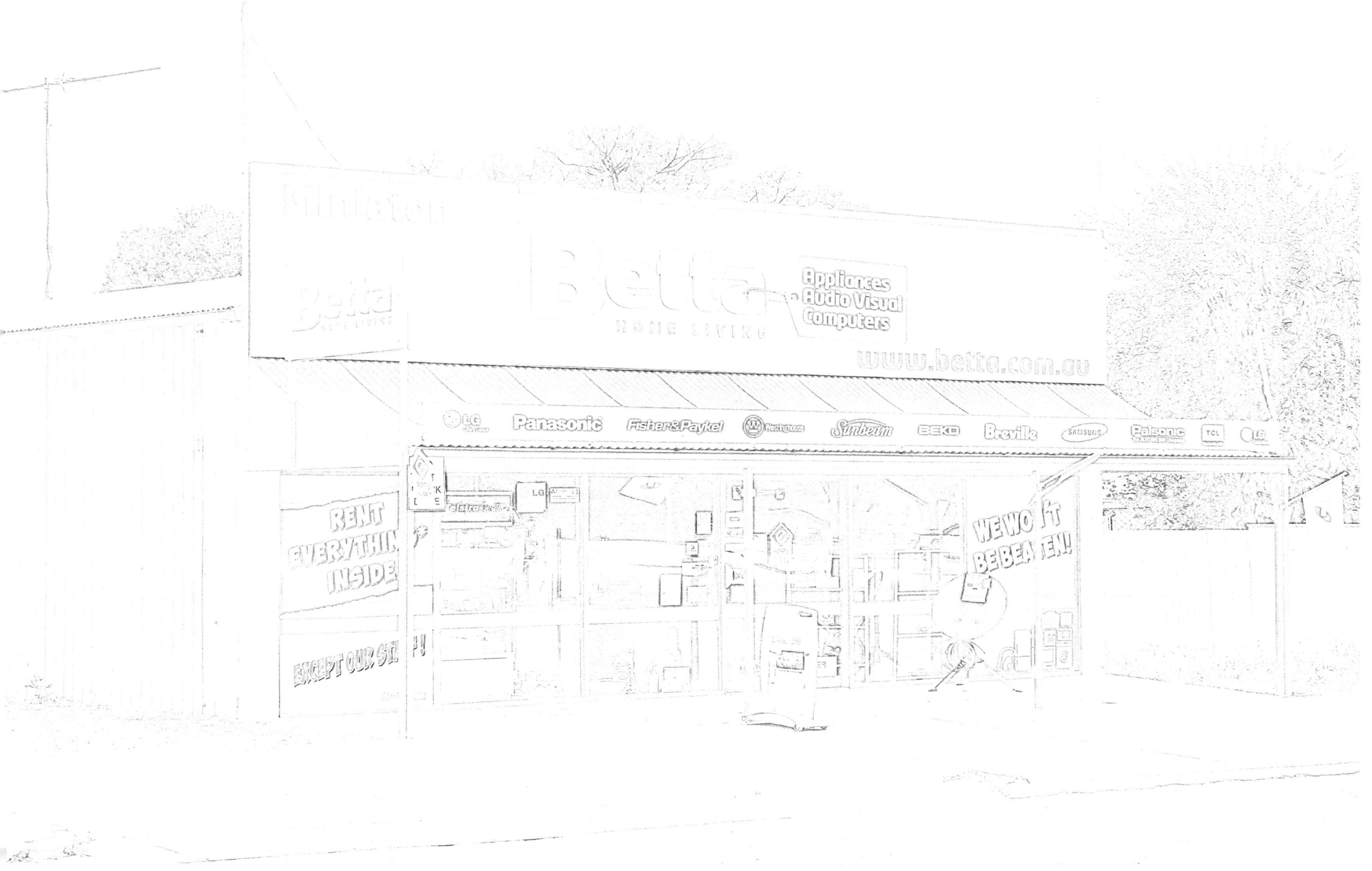
Minlaton
Betta
HOME LIVING
Betta
HOME LIVING
Appliances
Audio Visual
Computers
www.betta.com.au
LG
Panasonic
Fisher&Paykel
Westinghouse
Sunbeam
BEKO
Breville
SAMSUNG
TCL
LG
RENT
EVERYTHIN
INSIDE
EXCEPT OUR ST
WE WO T
BE BEA EN!

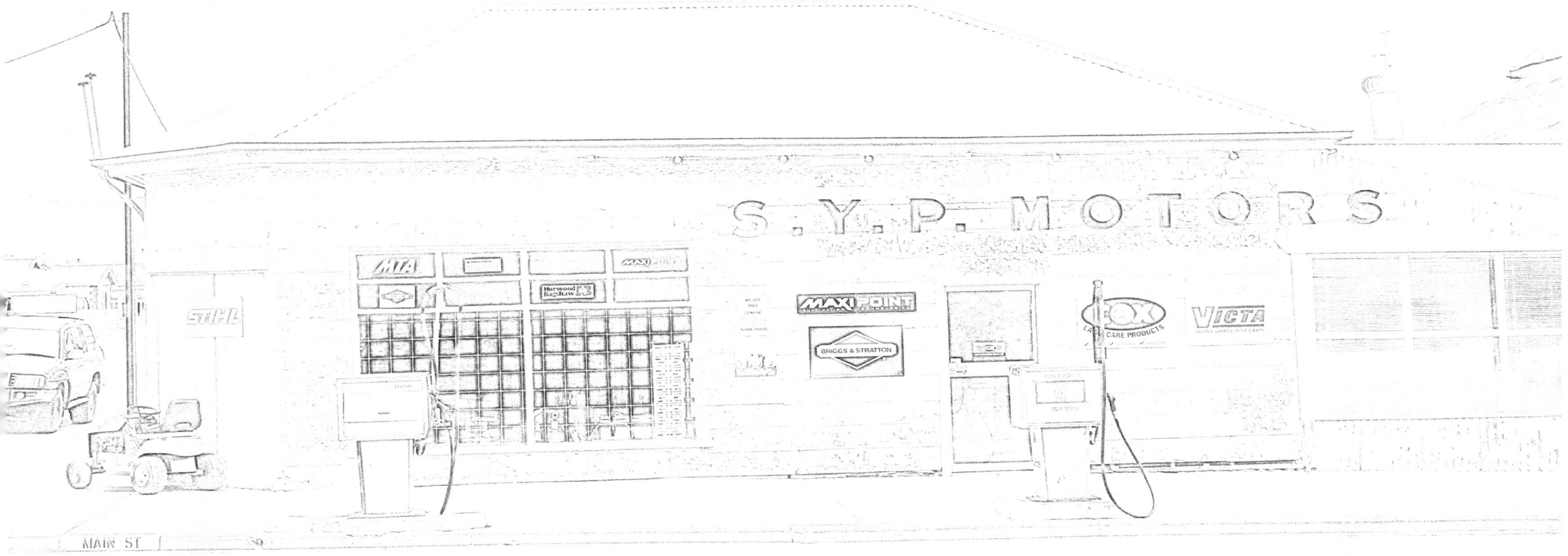
S.Y.P. MOTORS
MTA
Horwood Bagshaw
STIHL
MAXIPOINT
BRIGGS & STRATTON
CARE PRODUCTS
VICTA
MAIN ST

Catholic Church

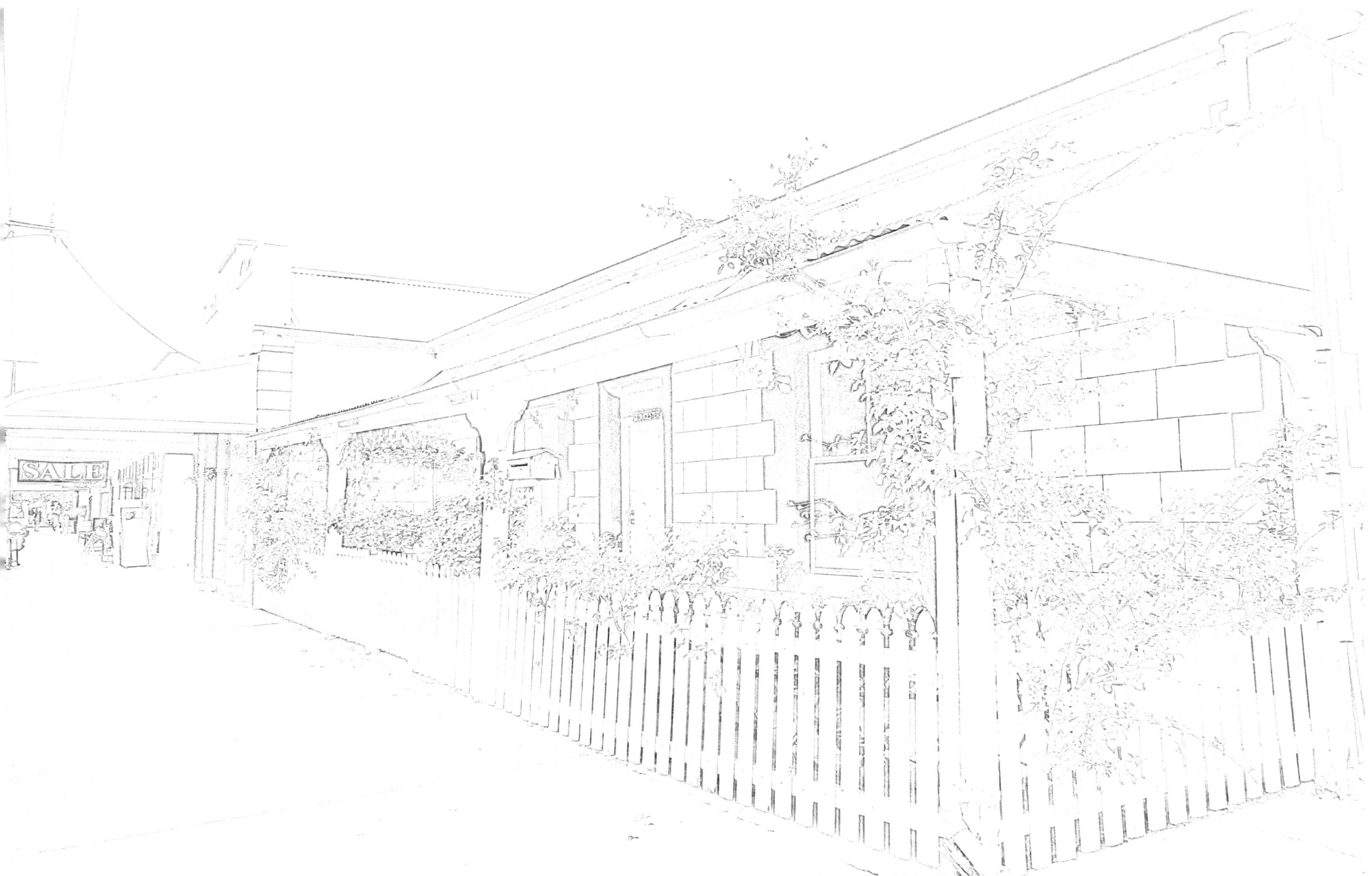
SALE

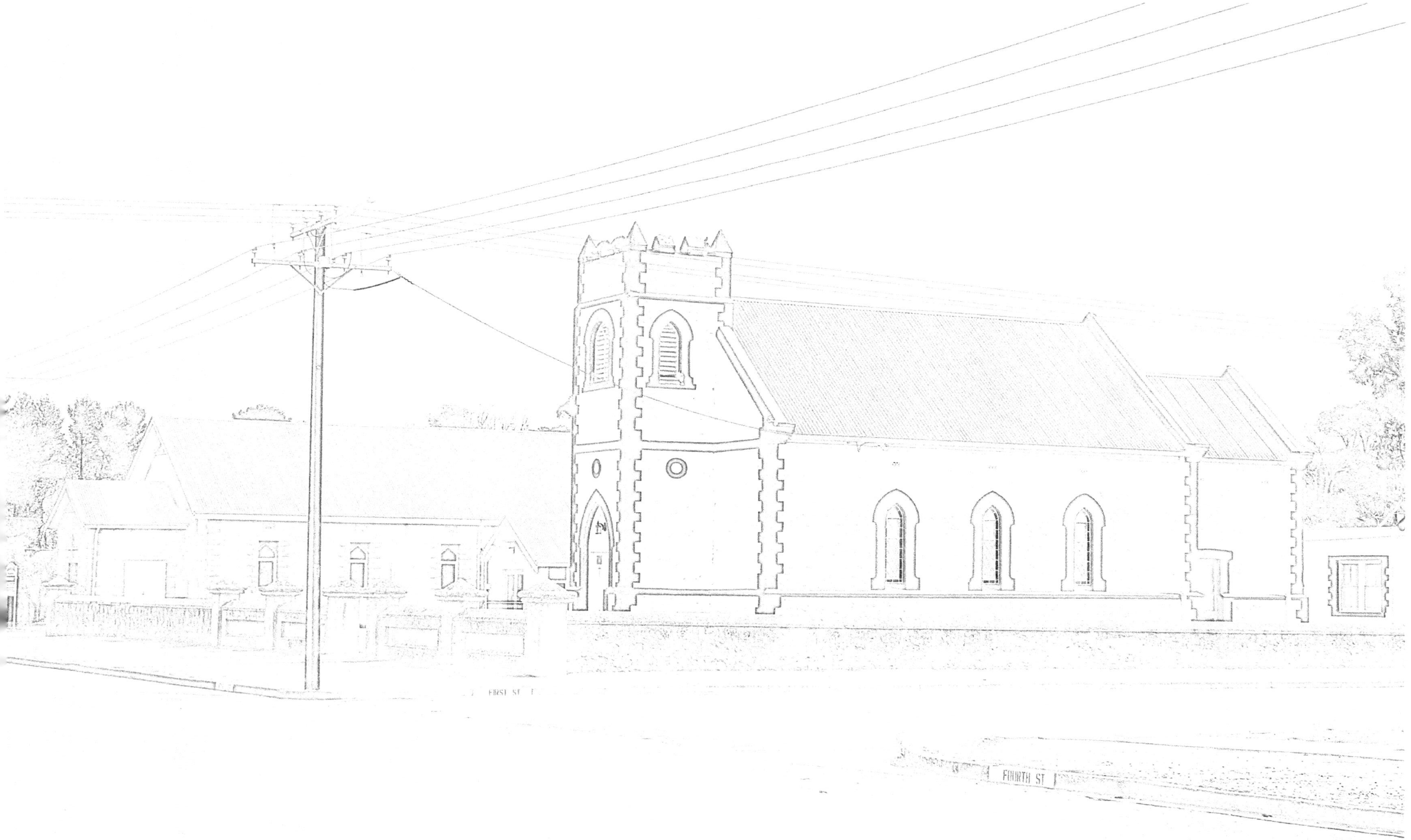
FIRST ST
FOURTH ST

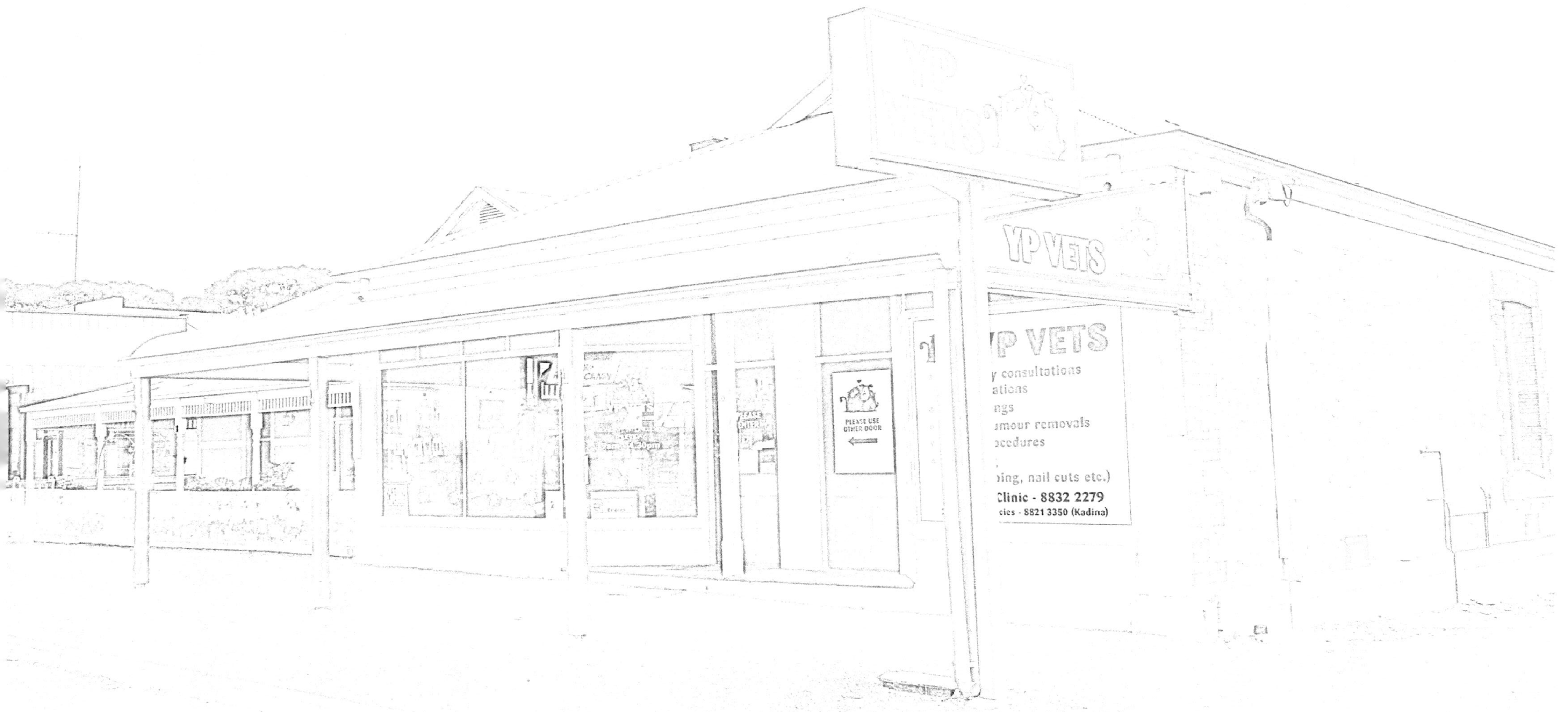

YP VETS
YP VETS
YP VETS
y consultations
ations
ngs
umour removals
ocedures
ping, nail cuts etc.)
Clinic - 8832 2279
cies - 8821 3350 (Kadina)
PLEASE USE OTHER DOOR

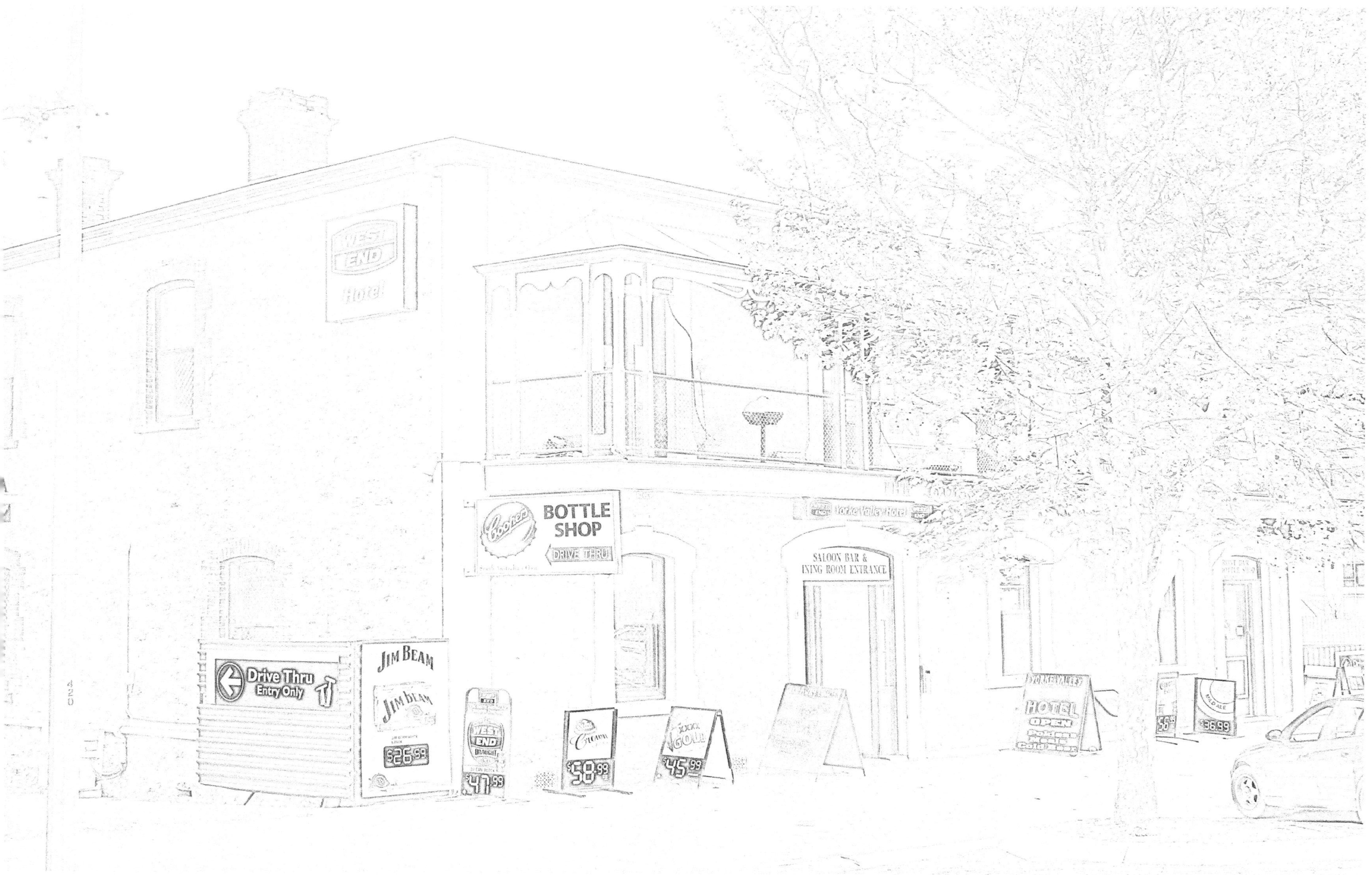

WEST END
Hotel
BOTTLE
SHOP
DRIVE THRU
SALOON BAR &
INING ROOM ENTRANCE
Yorke Valley Hotel
Drive Thru
Entry Only
JIM BEAM
$26.99
WEST END
DRAUGHT
$47.99
$58.99
$45.99
YORKE VALLEY
HOTEL
OPEN
$36.99

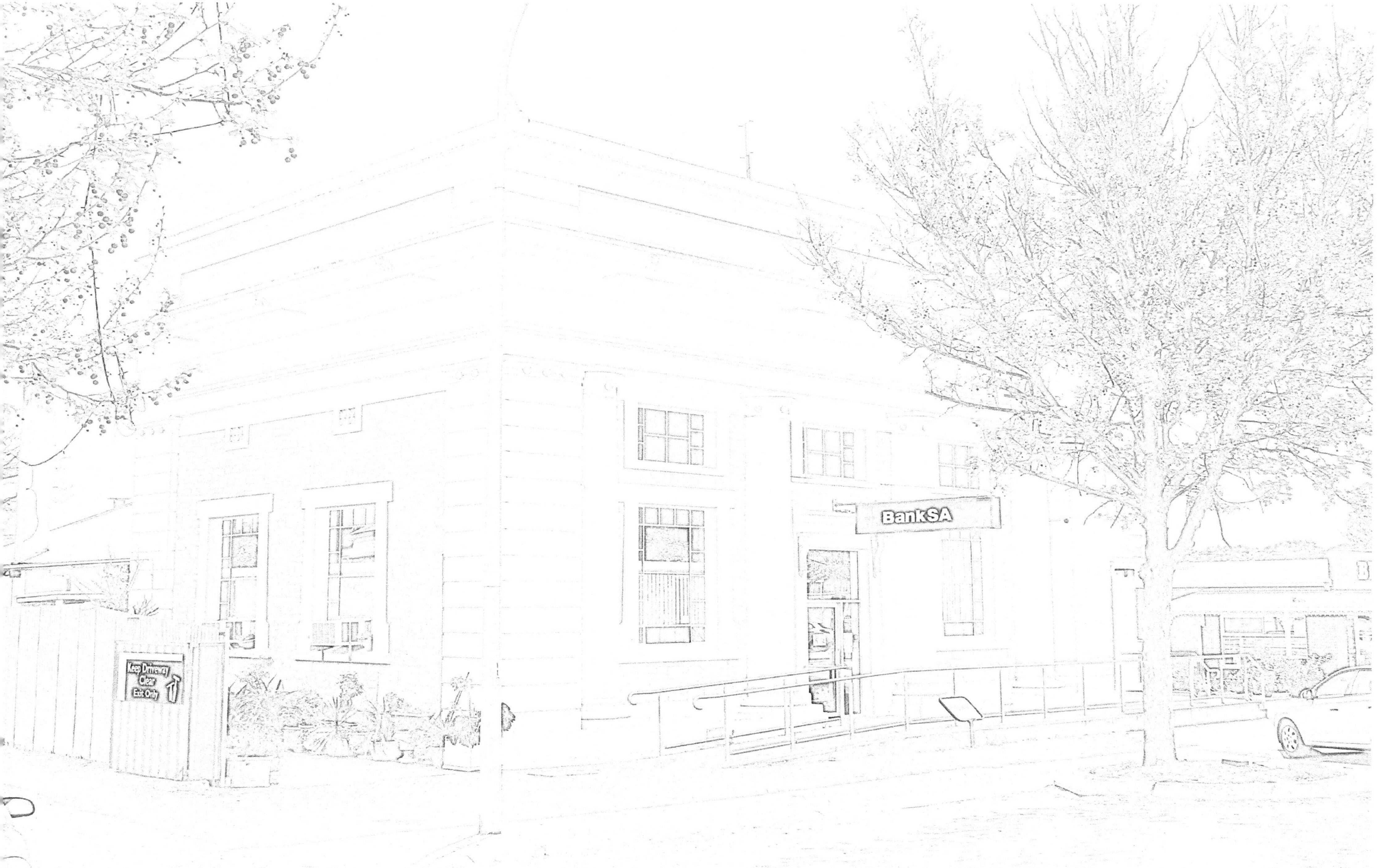
BankSA
Keep Driveway Clear
Exit Only

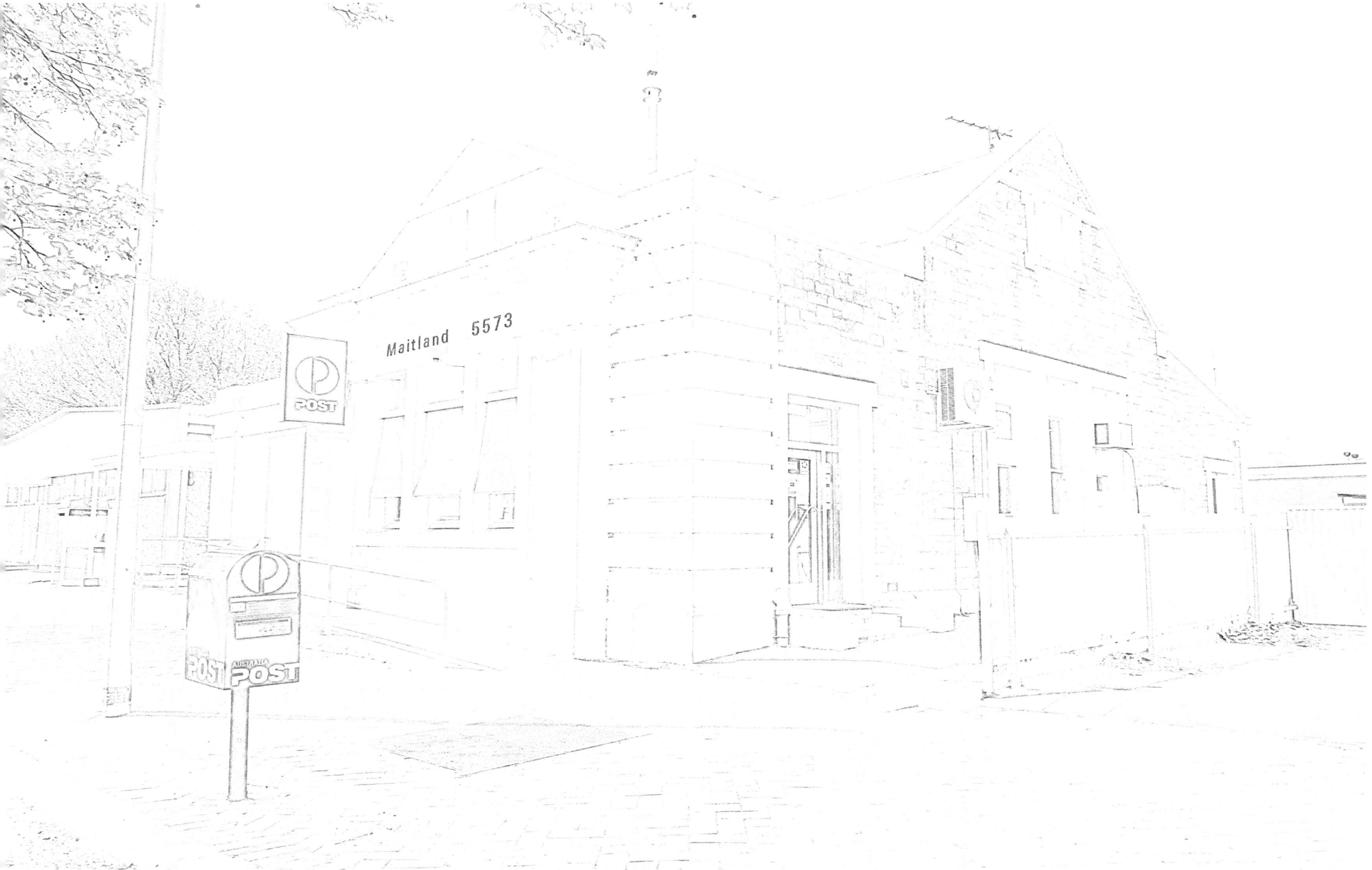
Maitland 5573
POST
AUSTRALIA POST
POST

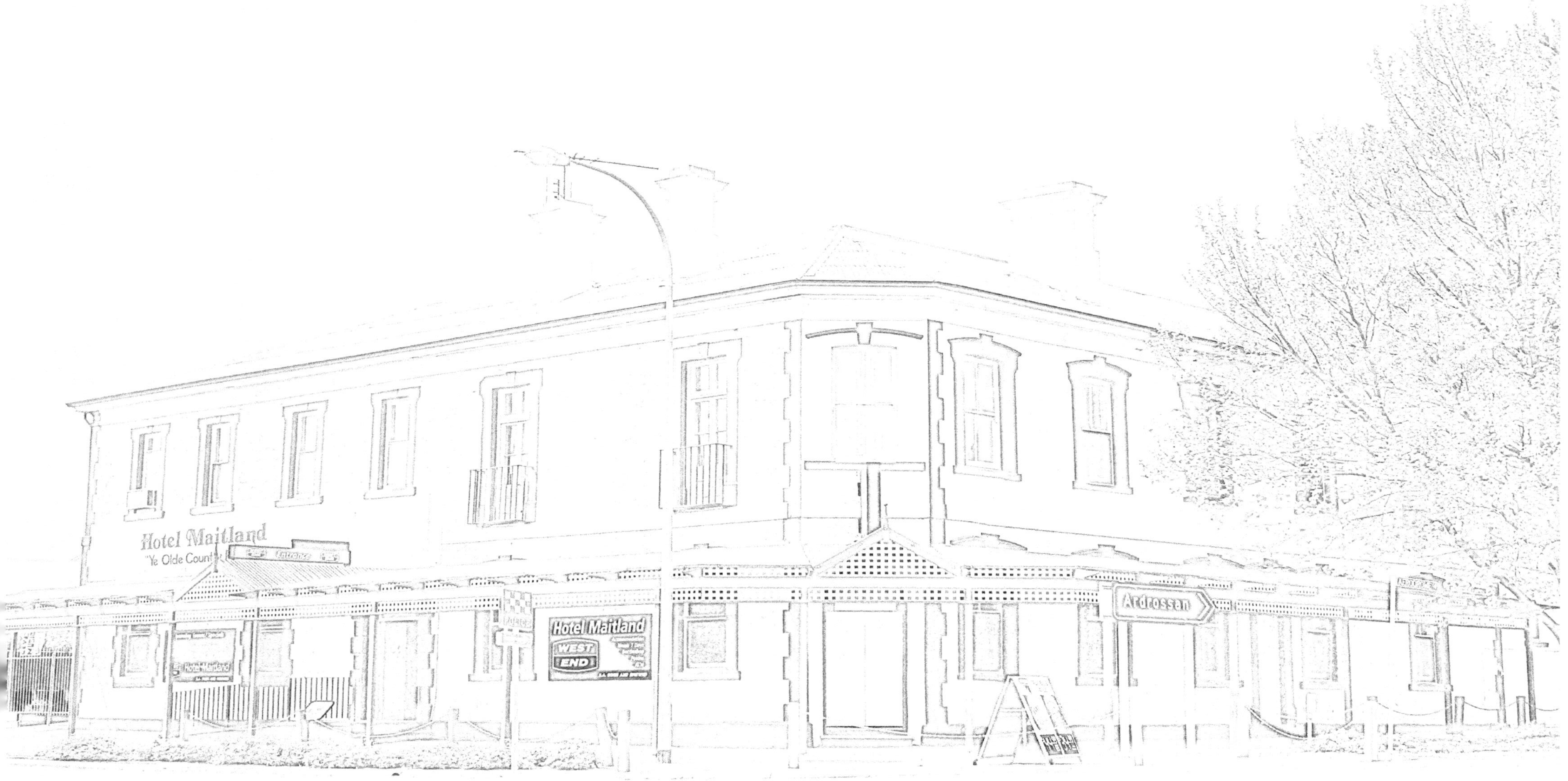
Hotel Maitland
"Ye Olde Count
Entrance
Hotel Maitland
WEST END
Ardrossan

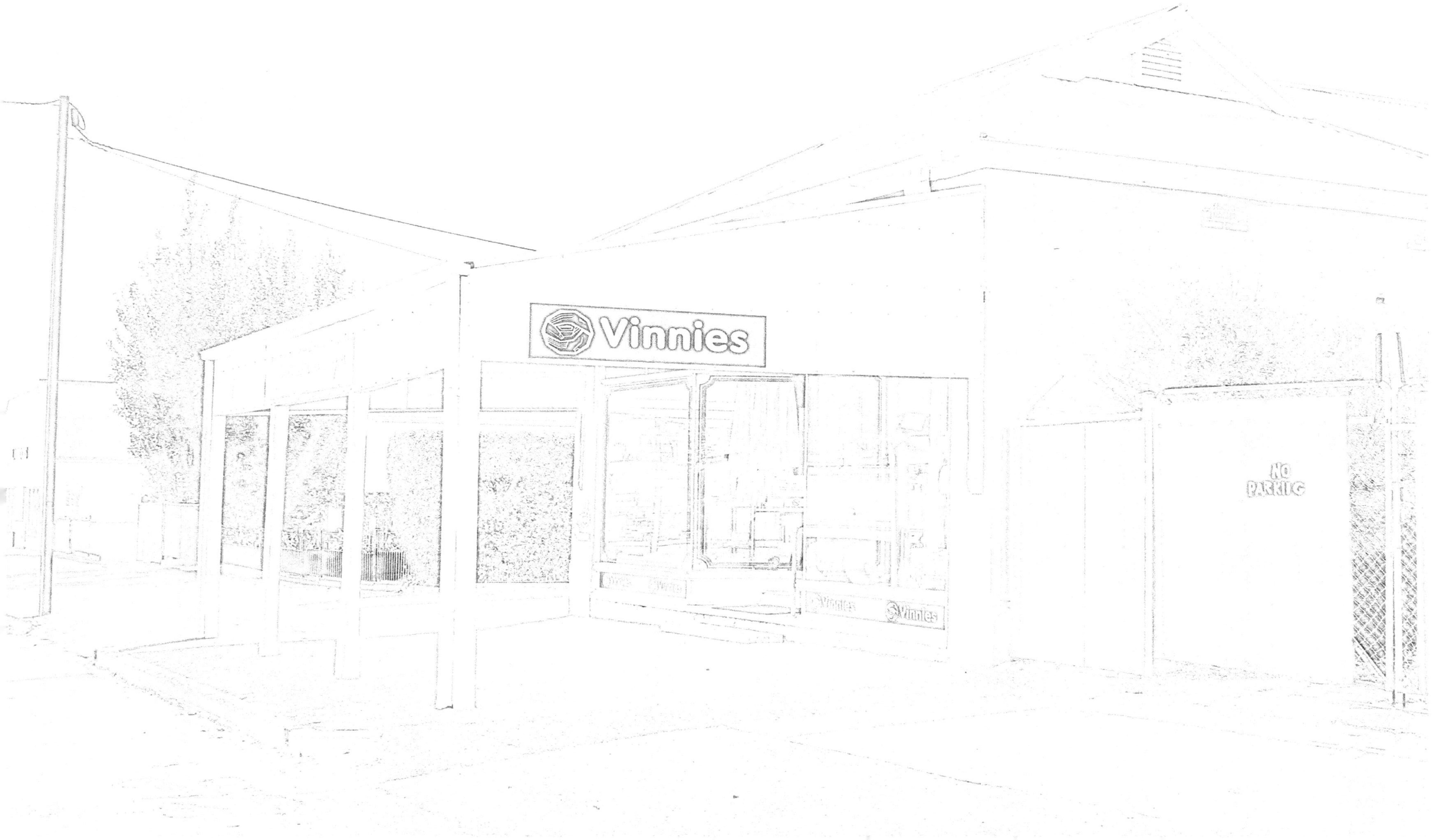
Vinnies
NO PARKING
Vinnies
Vinnies

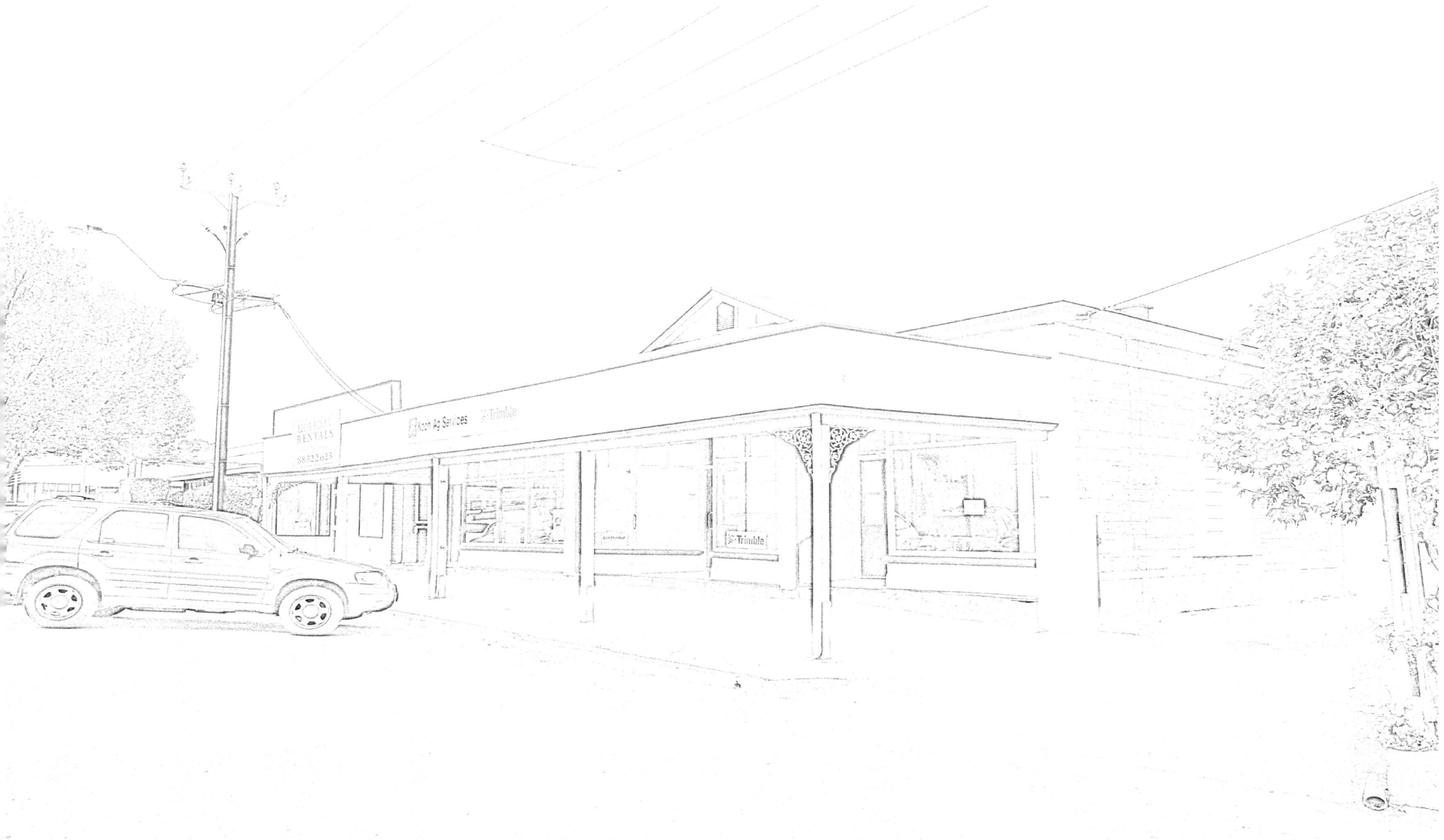

HOLIDAY
RENTALS
8822623
Koch Ag Services
Trimble
Trimble

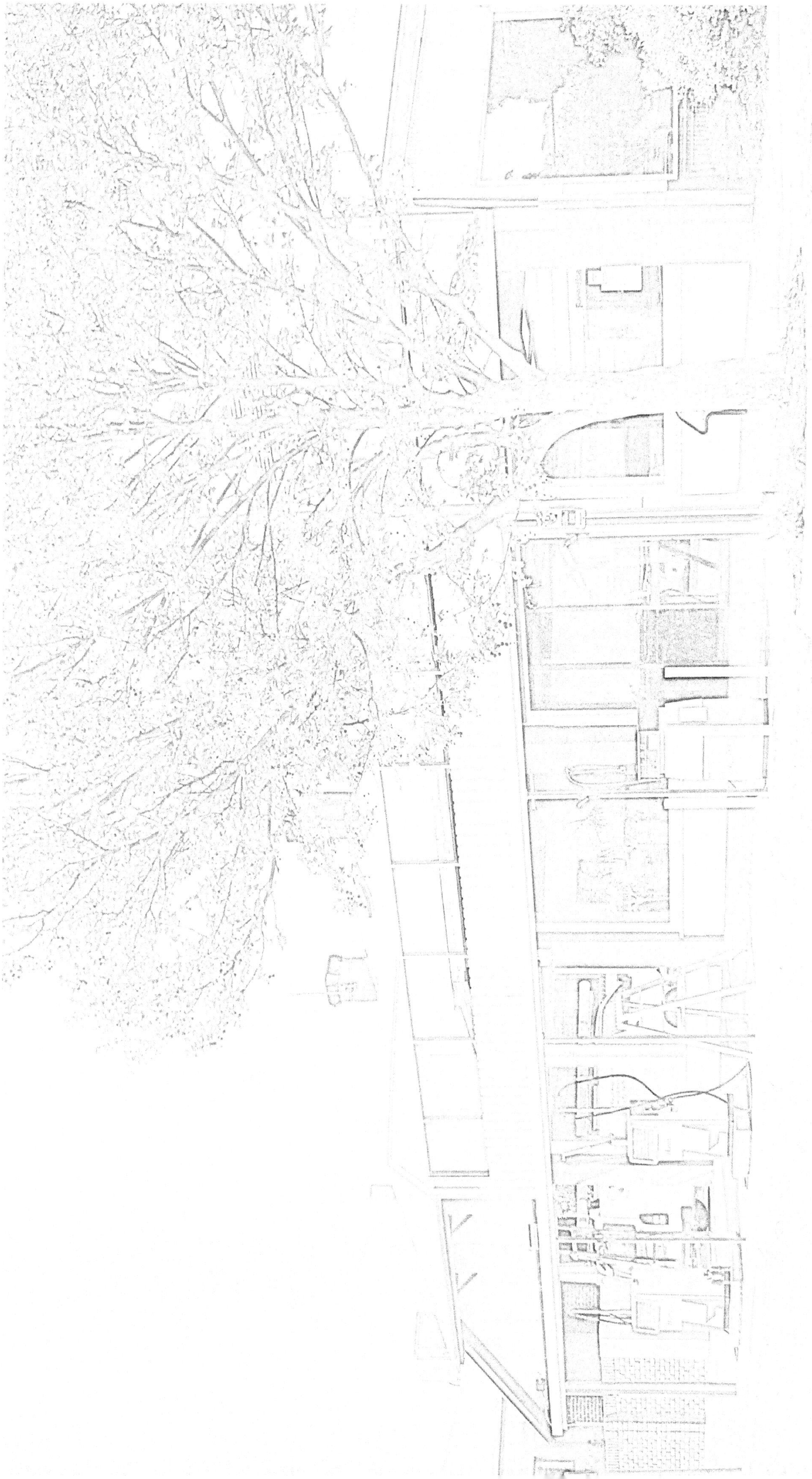

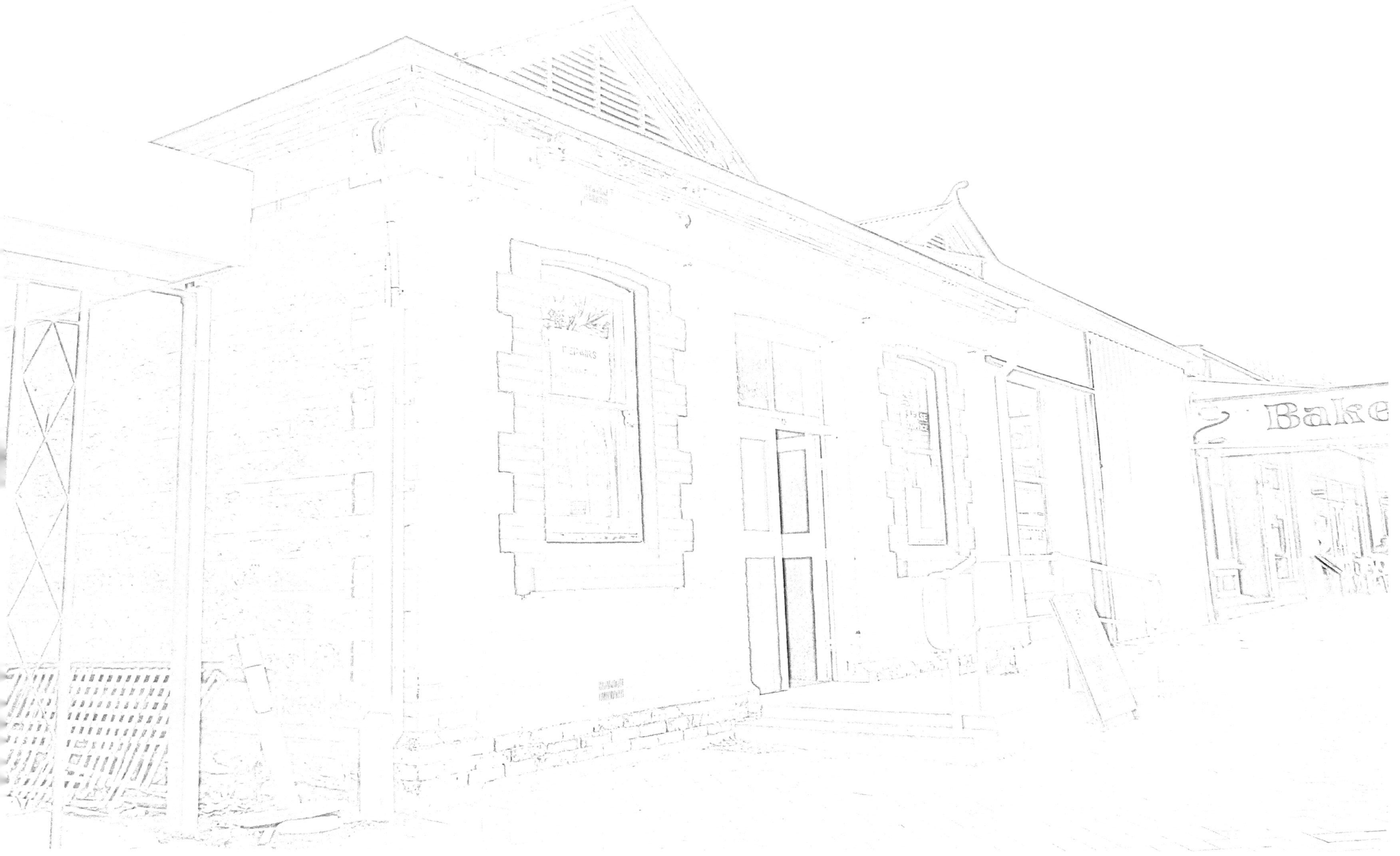
Bake

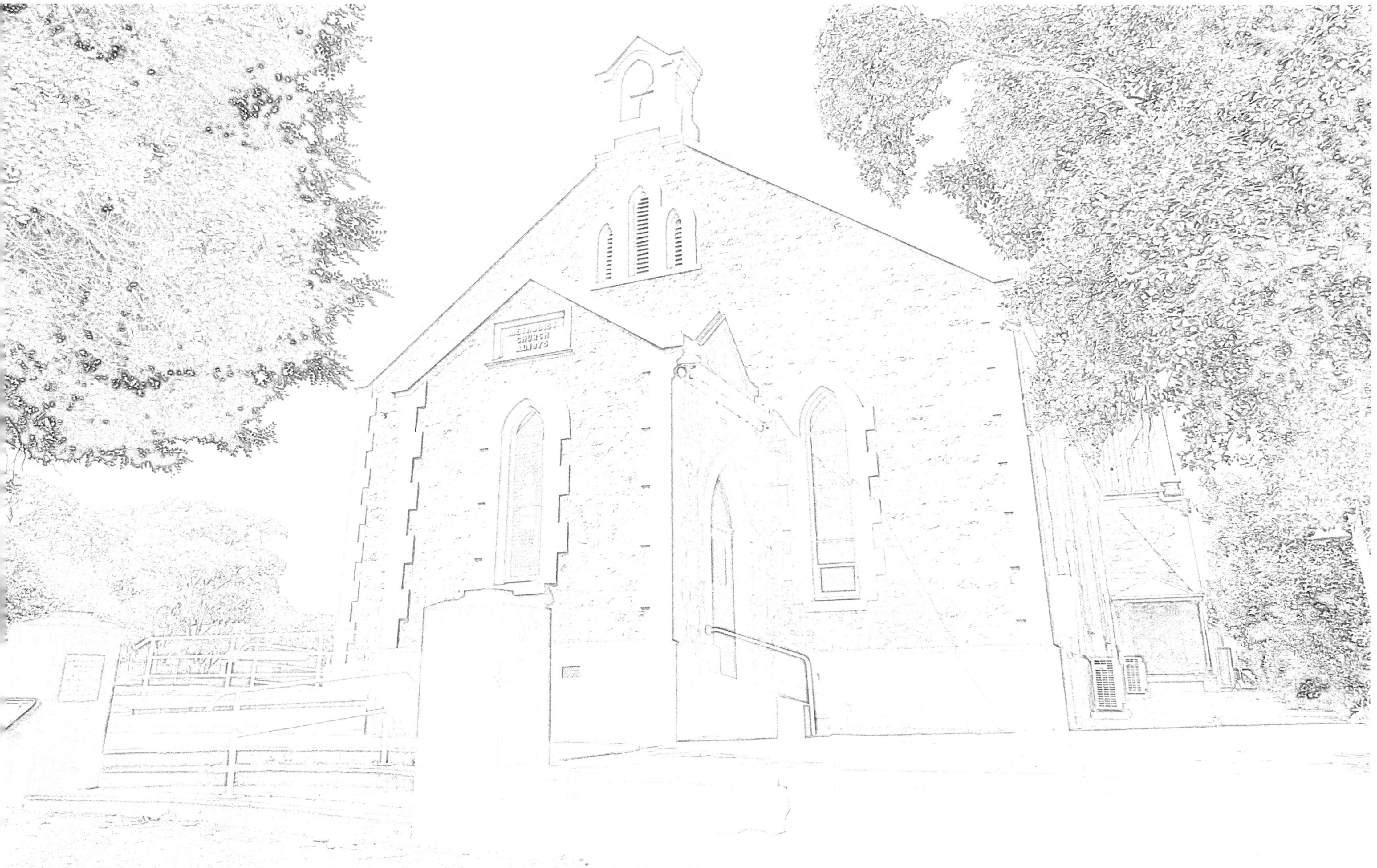
METHODIST
CHURCH
A.D.1879

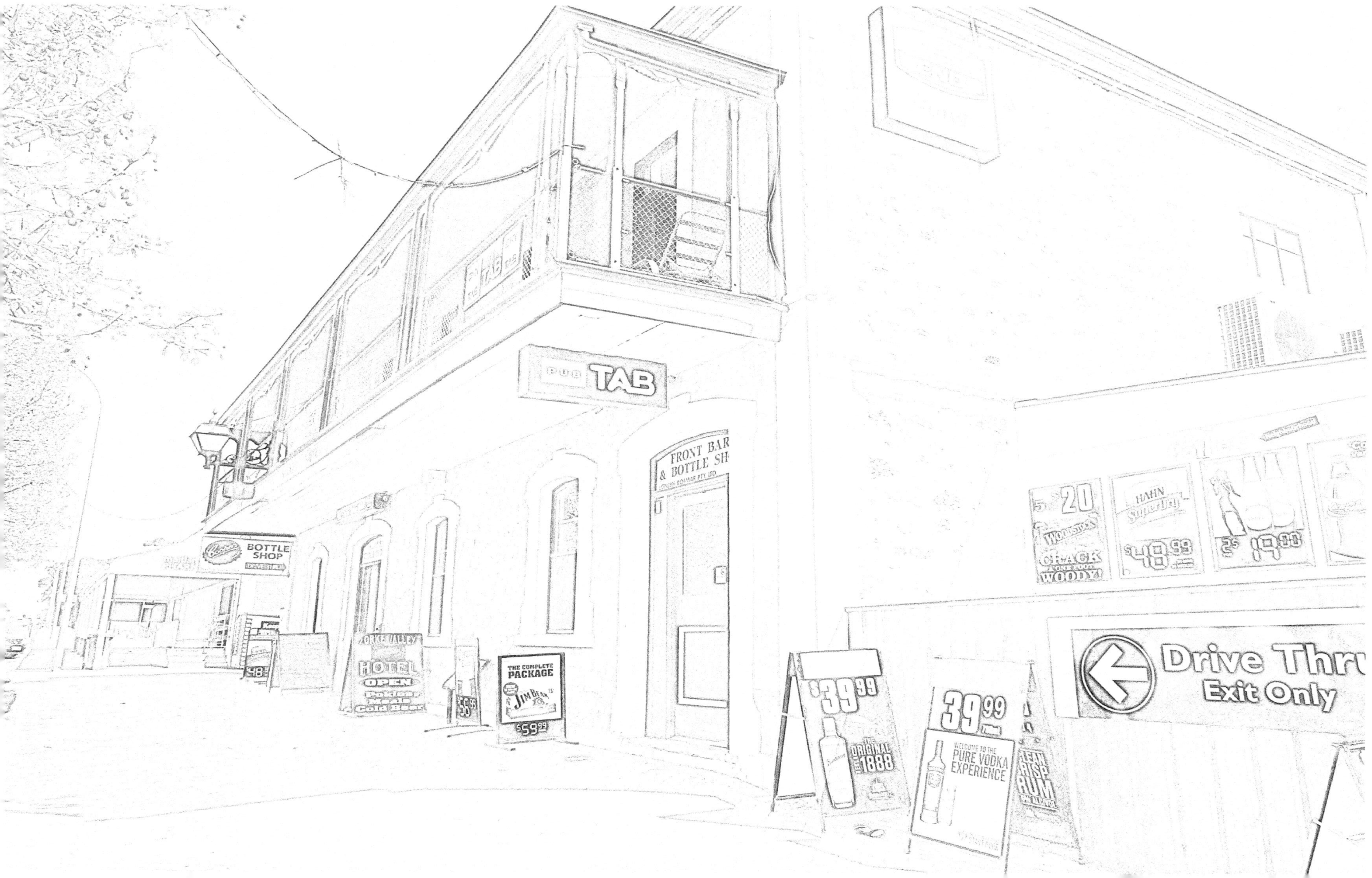
PUB TAB
FRONT BAR
& BOTTLE SHO
BOTTLE SHOP
DRIVE THRU
HOTEL
OPEN
Pokies
Meals
Cold Beer
THE COMPLETE PACKAGE
JIM BEAM
$59.99
$39.99
THE ORIGINAL 1888
39.99
WELCOME TO THE PURE VODKA EXPERIENCE
RUM
Drive Thru
Exit Only
$20
WOODSTOCK
CRACK
WOODY!
HAHN
$48.99
2s 19.98

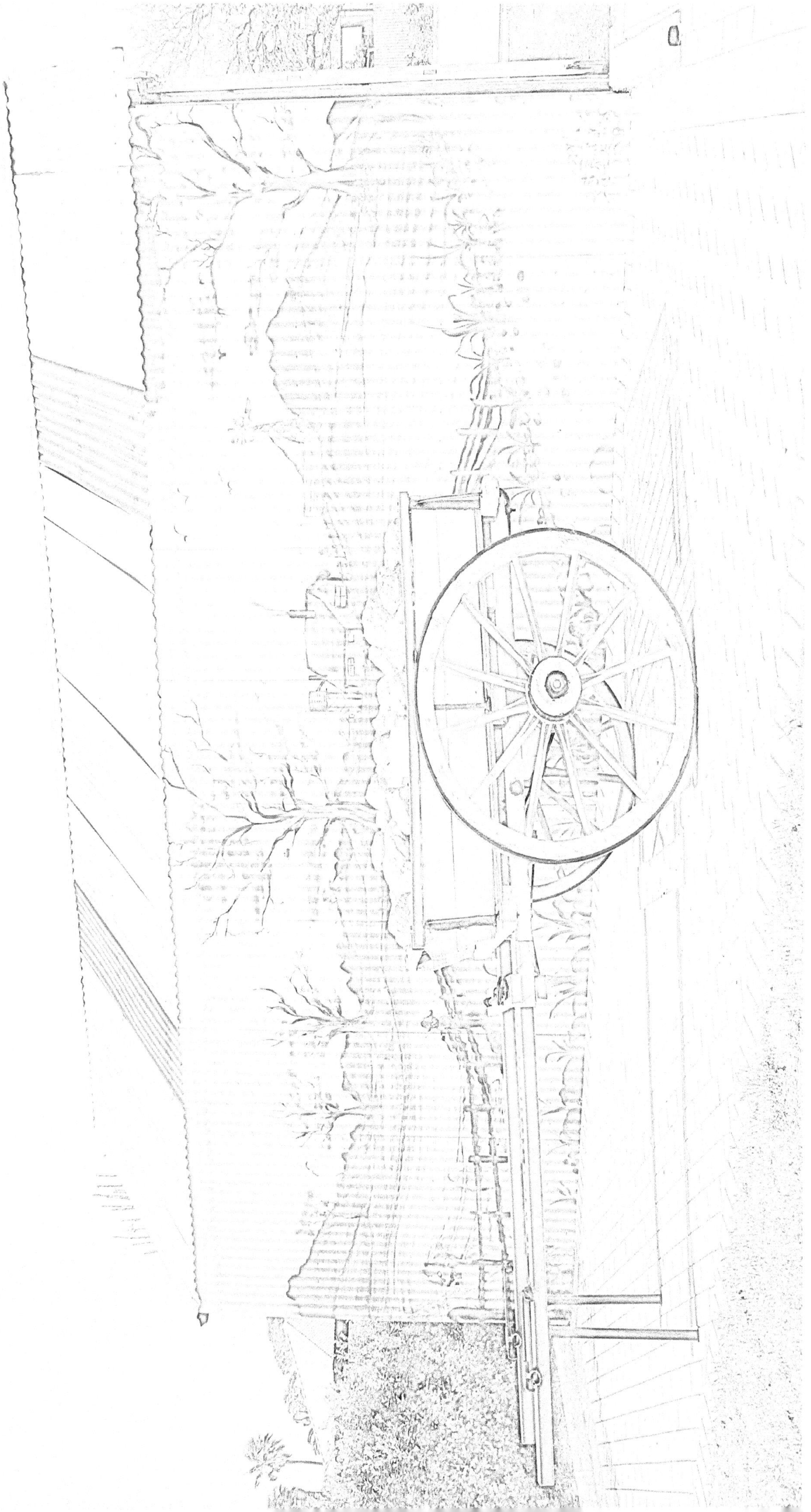

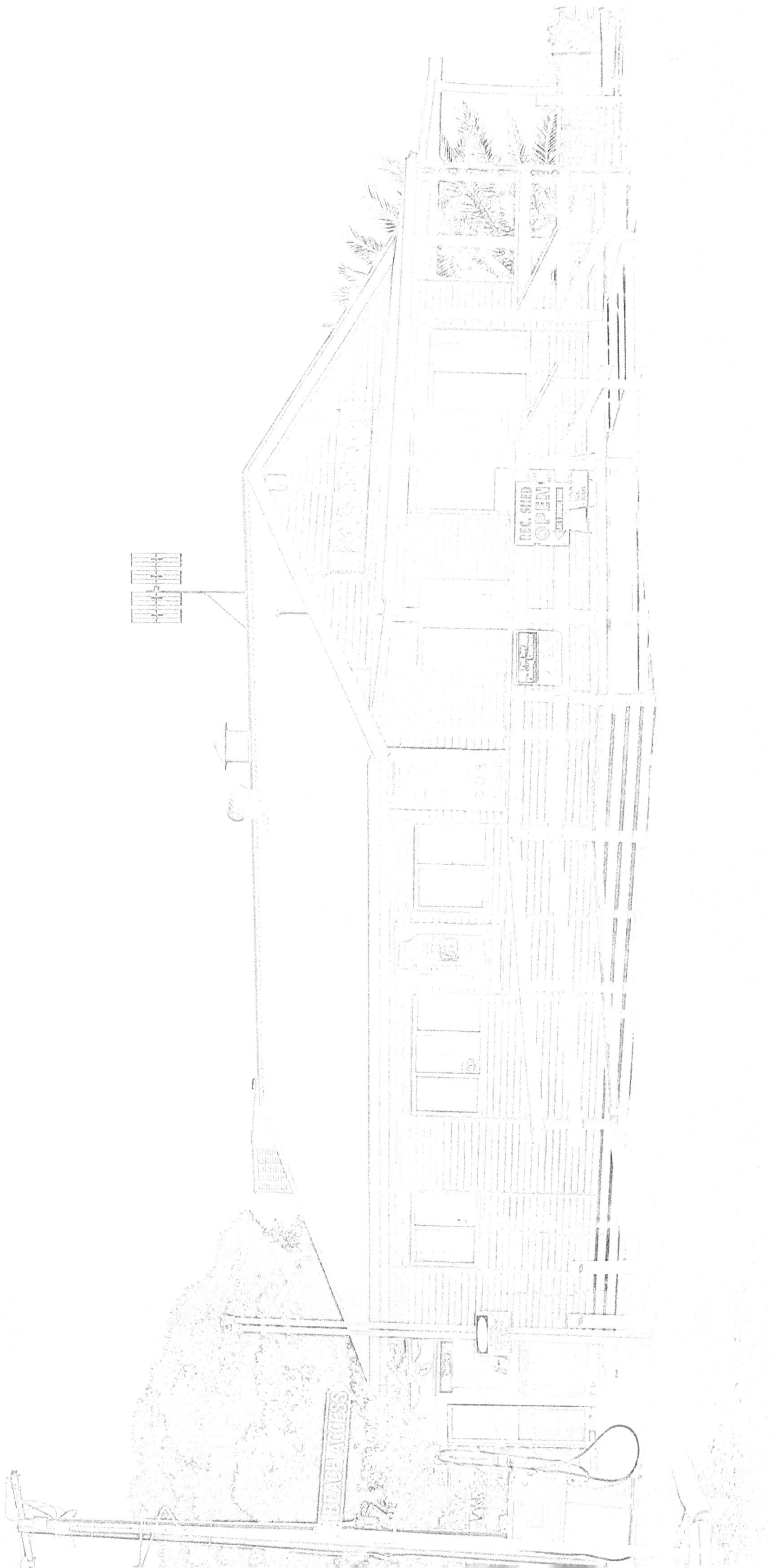
REC. SHED
OPEN
BEACH ACCESS

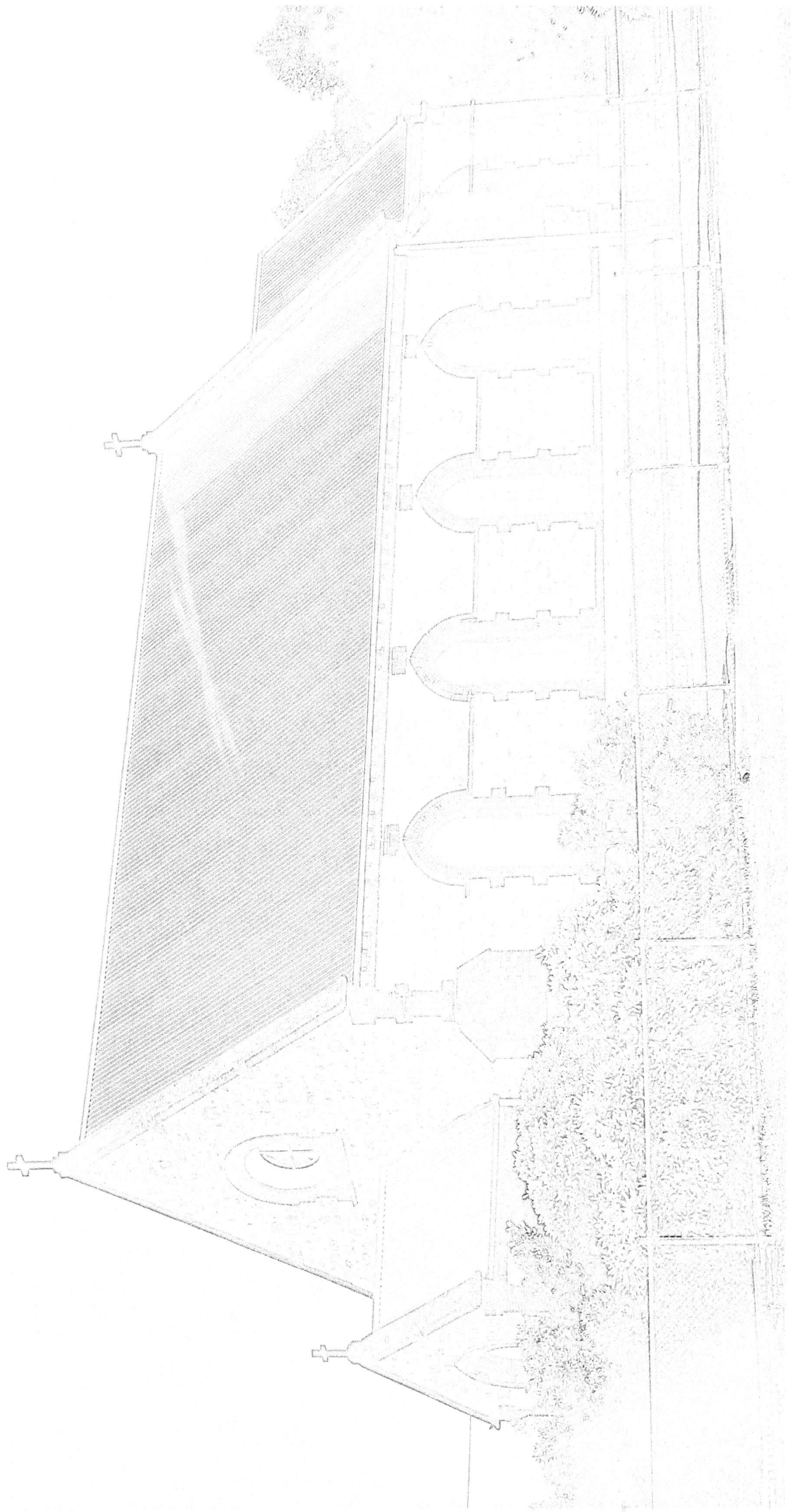

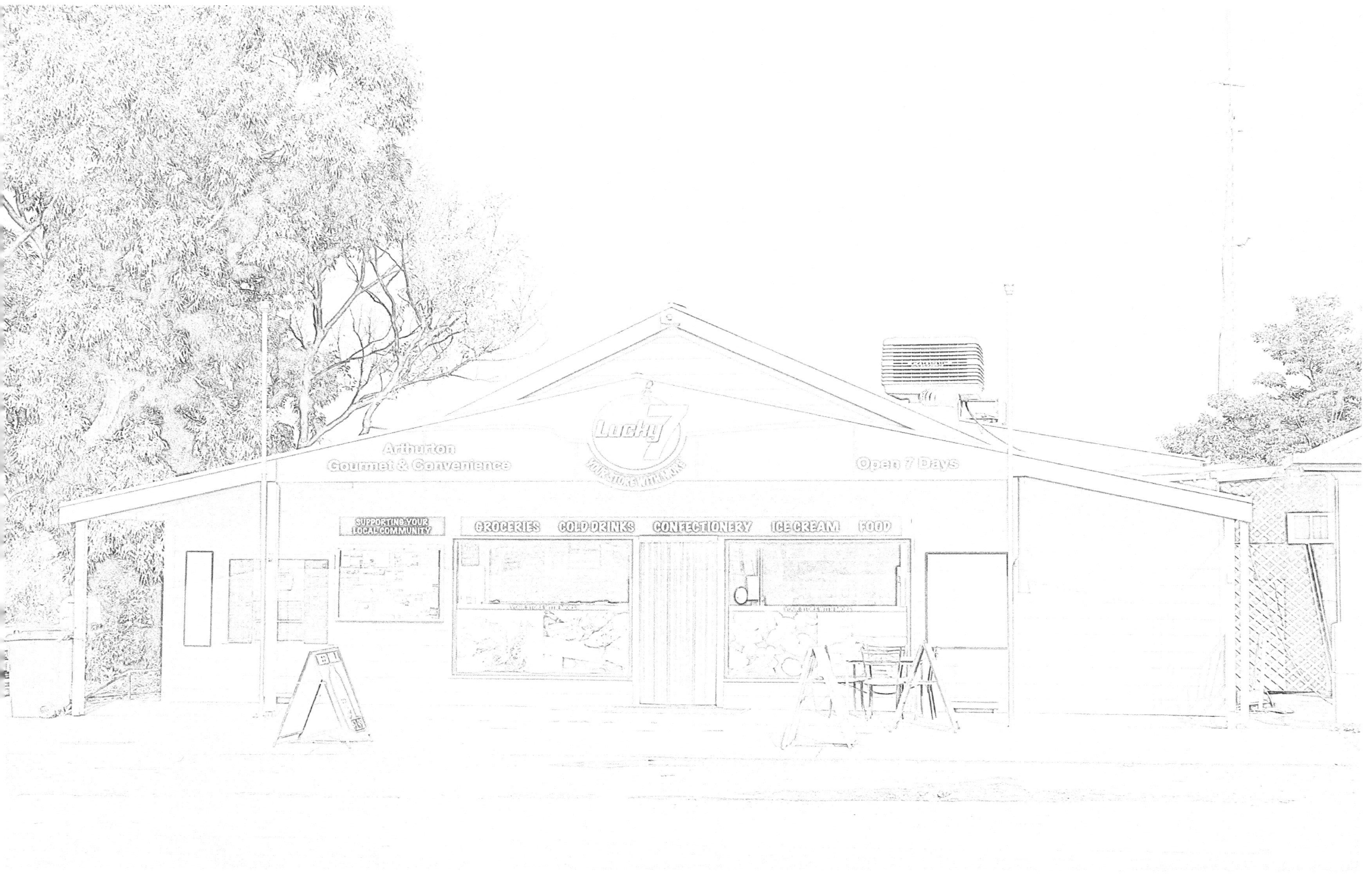

Arthurton
Gourmet & Convenience
Lucky 7
Open 7 Days
SUPPORTING YOUR LOCAL COMMUNITY
GROCERIES
COLD DRINKS
CONFECTIONERY
ICE CREAM
FOOD

SOLDIERS
MEMORIAL

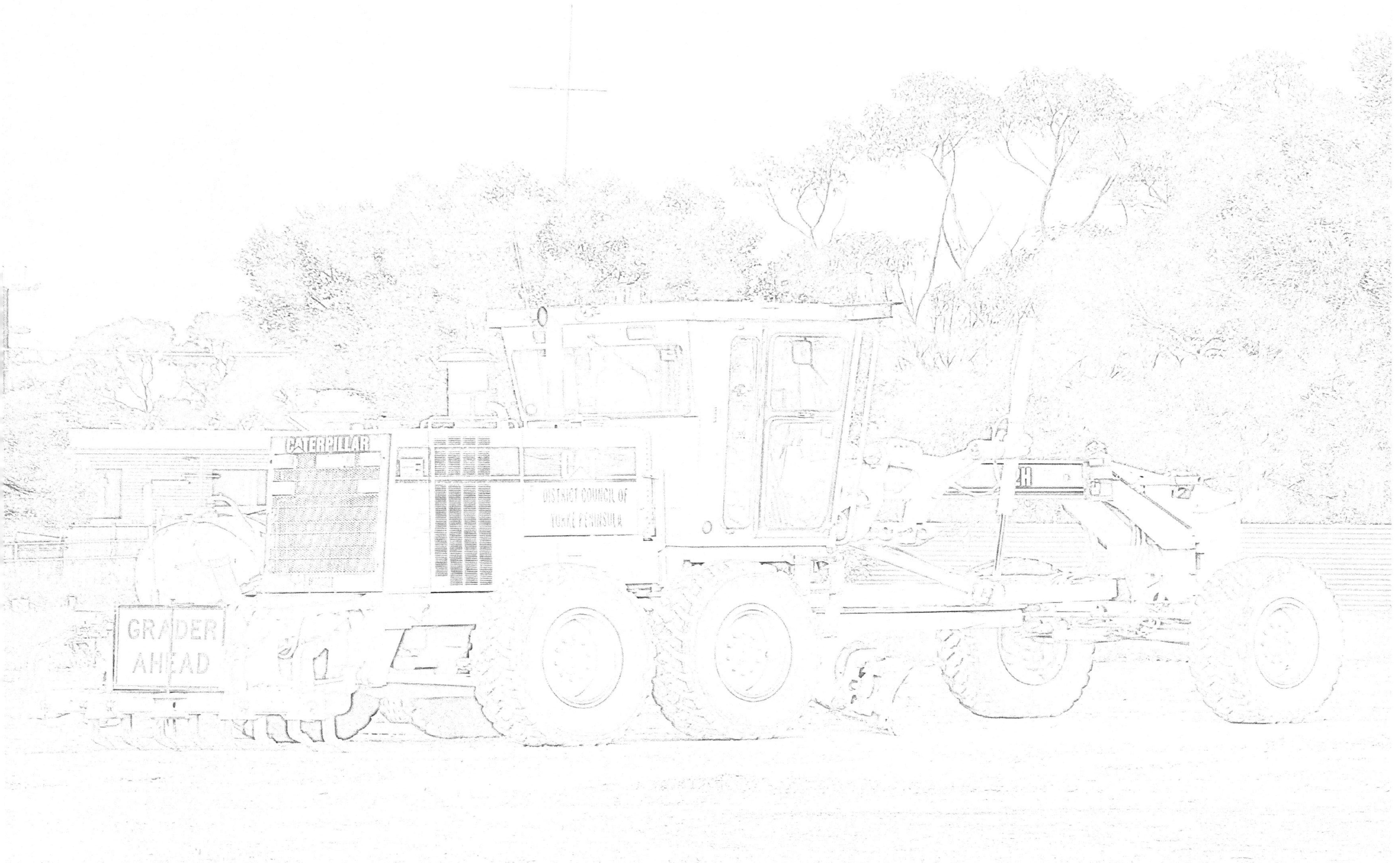
CATERPILLAR
DISTRICT COUNCIL OF
YORKE PENINSULA
GRADER
AHEAD

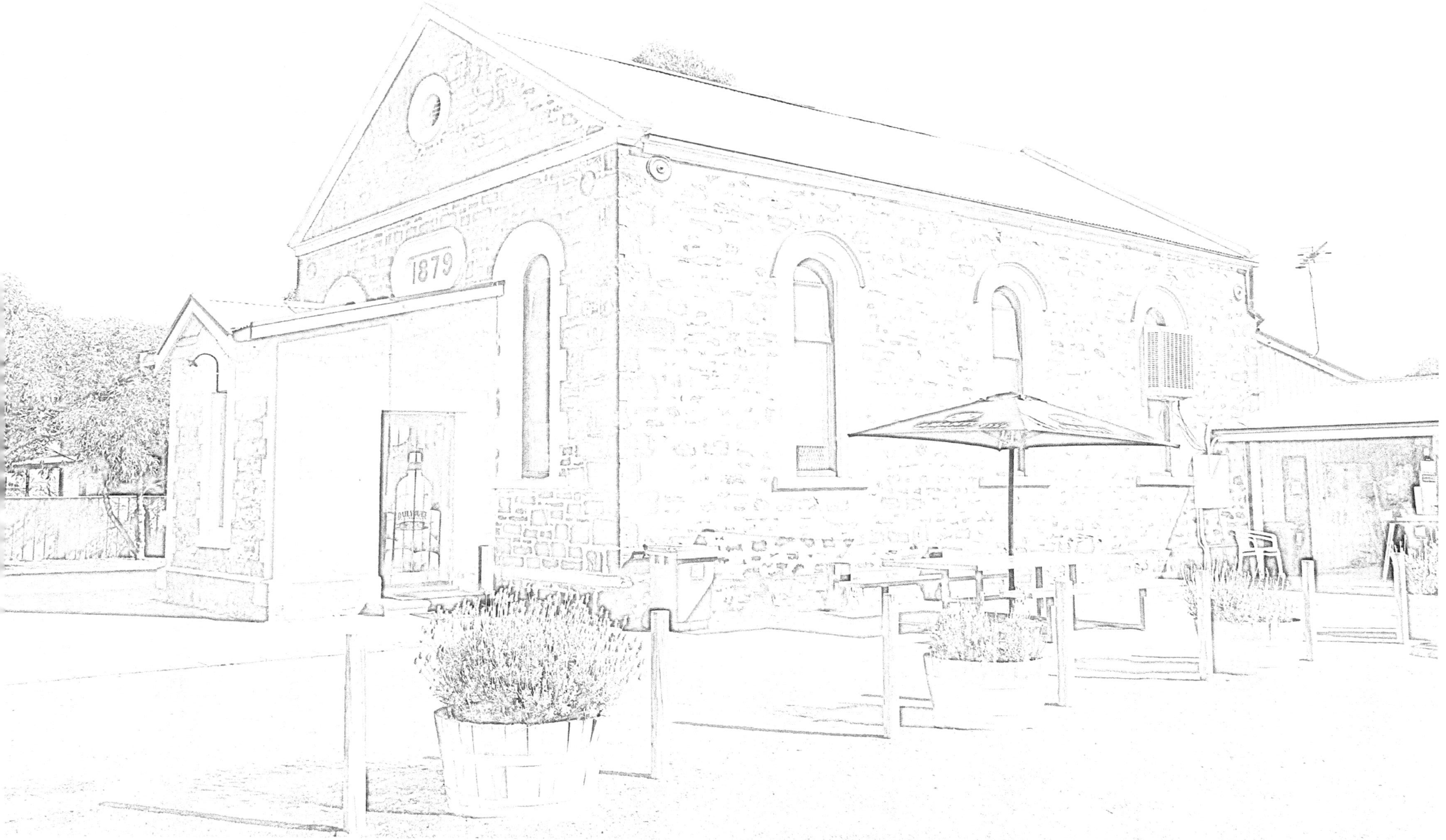
1879

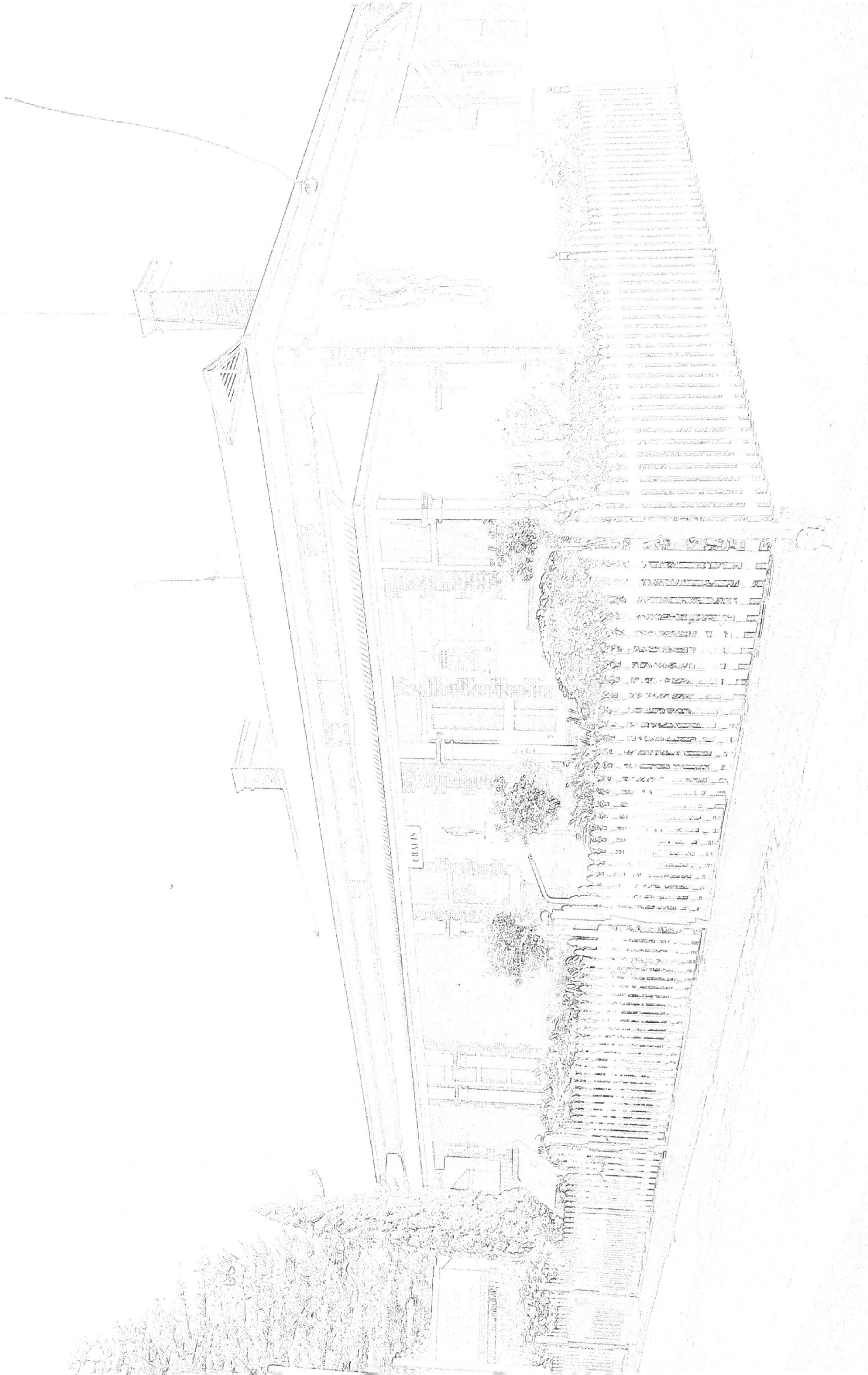

CRAFTS

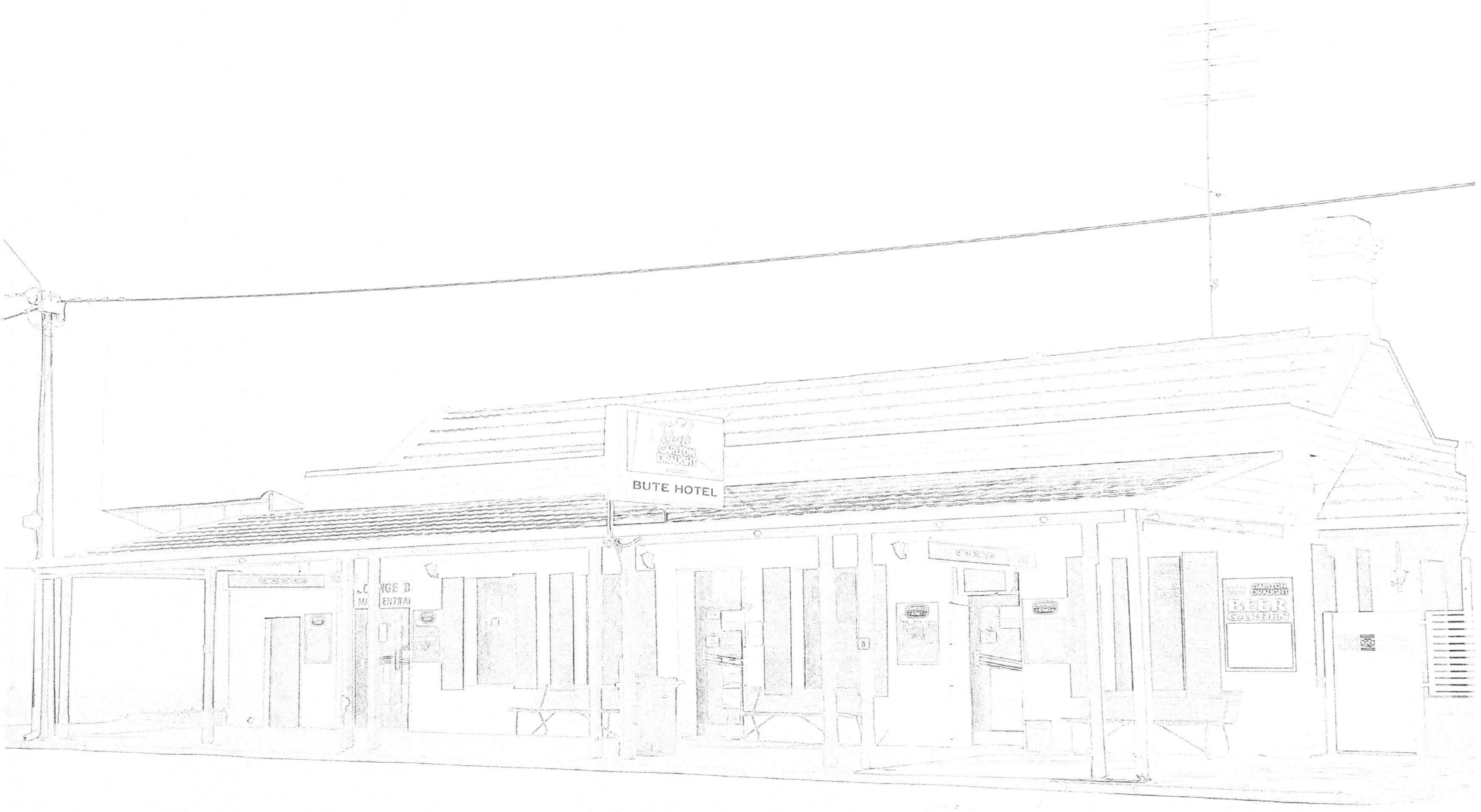
BUTE HOTEL
CARLTON DRAUGHT
CARLTON DRAUGHT
BEER GARDEN

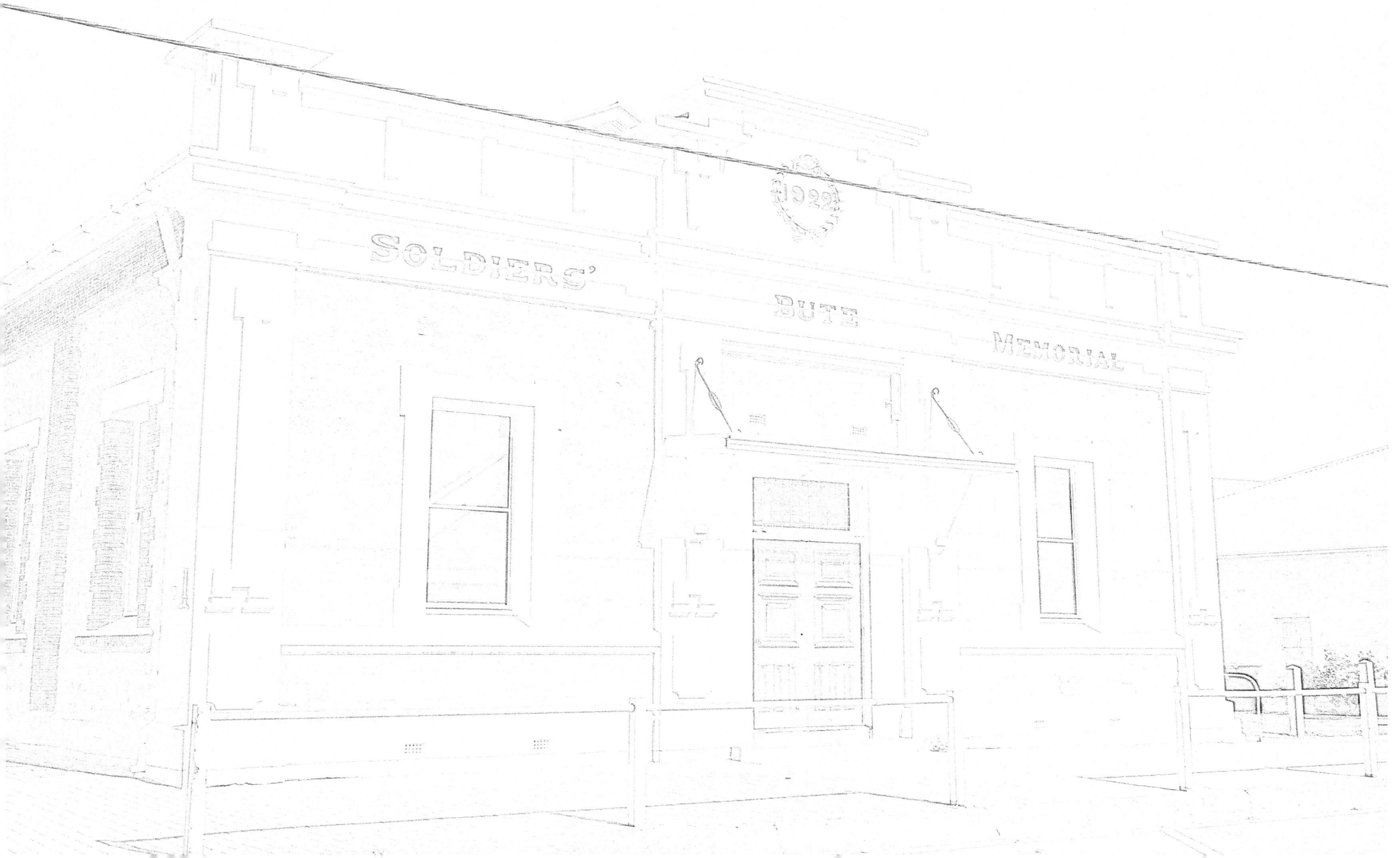
1922
SOLDIERS'
BUTE
MEMORIAL

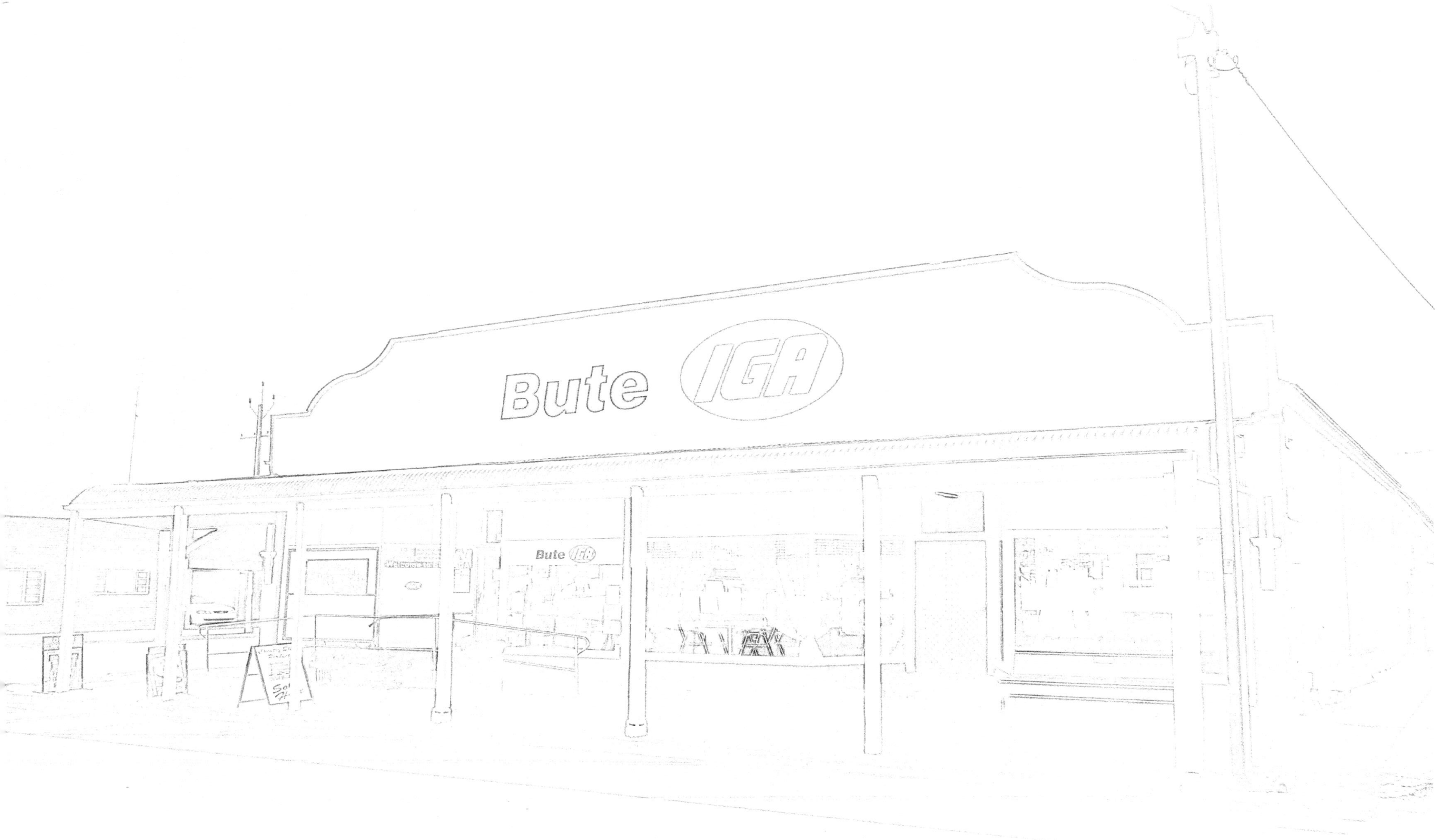
Bute IGA
Bute IGA

www.ingramcontent.com/pod-product-compliance
Lightning Source LLC
Chambersburg PA
CBHW081059180526
45170CB00005B/1810